Tombstones of
Roman Britain

Tombstones of Roman Britain

A Guide to Encountering the Dead

Stephanie Holton

First published in Great Britain in 2026 by
Pen & Sword History
An imprint of Pen & Sword Books Limited
Yorkshire – Philadelphia

Copyright © Stephanie Holton 2026

ISBN 978 1 03612 820 3

A CIP catalogue record for this book is
available from the British Library.

Typeset by Mac Style
Printed in the UK by CPI Group (UK) Ltd, Croydon, CR0 4YY.

The Publisher's authorised representative in the EU for product
safety is Authorised Rep Compliance Ltd., Ground Floor,
71 Lower Baggot Street, Dublin, D02 P593, Ireland.
www.arccompliance.com

For a complete list of Pen & Sword titles please contact:

PEN & SWORD BOOKS LIMITED
47 Church Street, Barnsley, South Yorkshire, S70 2AS, England
E-mail: enquiries@pen-and-sword.co.uk
Website: www.pen-and-sword.co.uk
or
PEN AND SWORD BOOKS
1950 Lawrence Road, Havertown, PA 19083, USA
E-mail: uspen-and-sword@casematepublishers.com
Website: www.penandswordbooks.com

AVIAE CARISSIMAE
VIXIT ANNOS LXXXII
S T T L

Contents

Acknowledgements

This little book arose from an outreach project I ran for several years called Romans on the Tyne. Based in the North East of England, the project introduced children to the ancient people who lived in and around the local area through the objects and inscriptions they left behind. Thanks to generous support from universities and charities I was able to run countless free workshops in schools and museums – including the fantastic Great North Museum: Hancock and Segedunum Roman Fort. The tombstones we investigated in these workshops always proved the most fascinating and the children loved the challenge of 'decoding' their hidden messages. After adapting the sessions for older audiences, I started working on the idea of creating a small guide to Roman tombstones for taphophiles of all ages who might like to venture to their local museum or fort and meet their Roman-era residents.

I am especially grateful to the many wonderful museum educators and curators who are always willing to share not only their time but also their enthusiasm for the ancient past – especially Morgan Fail, Kirsty Robinson, Andrew Parkin, Alex Croom, and all the members of the Hadrian's Wall Learning and Engagement Forum. I'm also fortunate to find myself among kind and supportive colleagues at The Open University: many sections of this book were written in their company at writing retreats and collaborative working sessions.

Finally, a special mention goes to my ever-patient son Hector, who accompanied me on a summer train odyssey through Roman Britain to photograph many of the tombstones you will encounter in this book. We explored everything from wild ruins, cathedral crypts, pub basements and windswept crags to museums of all shapes and sizes – acquiring many toy swords, shields and pencils from the countless gift shops along the way.

Introduction

The ancients took great care to honour and remember their dead. There was little of the avoidance that we have developed in our modern Western world around death and all that comes with it. Dying was, after all, a very common part of ancient life. For the Greeks and the Romans, proper care of the deceased was an important responsibility for the living. Memory was a means of immortality for mortals, as a name could long outlast a physical body. Without loved ones or comrades to give you the proper funerary rites after death, your soul – the intangible bit of you that survives the physical body's demise – would not be able to gain access to the underworld. As the poet Virgil tells us, the souls of those whose bodily remains were not laid to rest littered the banks of the river Styx, as innumerable as autumn leaves, unable to cross with the ferryman and gain entrance to the world of the dead.[1] It is perhaps not surprising then that many men and women across Roman society joined burial clubs into which they regularly paid contributions.[2] This was not dissimilar to a modern-day funeral plan: through these regular payments, the cost of the funeral would then be covered after death, allowing the individual to take comfort in the knowledge their body – and their soul – would be properly laid to rest after they themselves were gone.

Roman care for the dead closely followed the long-established practices of the Ancient Greeks. For the many deaths that did not happen away at war, the deceased would be brought back to the house. Family members – or, for the wealthy, employees of the undertaker – would wash and anoint the body, then dress it in clean white clothes. In the case of male Roman citizens, the body was dressed in the toga to symbolise their status even in death. The head of the deceased was often crowned with a wreath, and a small coin placed in the mouth to pay the ferryman Charon's fee to cross the river Styx.[3] Some accounts describe the body being placed with the feet towards the door. Family and friends would gather around the body to share stories and sing songs about their loved one as well as express their own grief and loss. Across Roman artistic and literary sources, women are often depicted tearing their hair or scratching their faces in acts of mourning.

On the eighth day after death, the body would be carried from the house on a bier in a funeral procession to the site of either burial or cremation. This took place at night and was a noisy affair, with musicians and mourners (dressed in black) accompanying the procession. The deceased's remains were then interred in a cemetery and a grave marker was erected on their final resting place. These markers varied greatly in shape and style across the Roman world, from elaborately decorated marble sarcophagi and elegant tombs to columbaria and roughly hewn stones bearing only a name. The Law of the Twelve Tables did not allow burial to take place within the walls of a town: thus, Roman cemeteries were usually placed outside of a settlement, lining the roads between towns and cities. In this way, the dead were not tucked away but rather, prominently placed by the roadside. Colourfully painted tombstones featuring portraits and many other kinds of lively scenes gazed out at the traveller as they passed, while the many inscribed epitaphs sometimes even addressed the passer-by directly, offering guidance from beyond the grave on how to make the most of life while still living.

The burial was not the end for the deceased. Honouring and remembering the dead was a significant part of Roman culture, both in private family practice and in wider public religious activities. Having returned from the funeral, the family carried out purification rites and held the funerary banquet (*silicernium*) to honour the deceased. They would regularly visit the grave to leave gifts and offerings for the dead, especially on the deceased's birthday. There were also civic festivals that focused on the dead such as the *Parentalia*, which honoured ancestors and the spirits of the dead (the *di Manes*), and the *Lemuria*, which warded off any restless ghosts.

As the vast Roman Empire expanded further, these long-held customs and traditions were brought to new and unfamiliar lands. Following the initial invasion of AD 43, the Romans incorporated the island of Britannia into their sprawling empire as a province. Conquest was not instant: it took many years for the army to progress through the territories and subdue or secure the many different Celtic tribes who ruled their own regions.[4] Throughout the 400 years of occupation that followed, the province experienced the impact of Romanisation across all facets of life – from administration to architecture, economy to agriculture, religion to communication – and a strong Romano-British culture and identity emerged. The beliefs and practices around death and the dead reflected this, incorporating not just new Roman ideas about the treatment of the corpse but also new methods of commemoration – including, vitally for this book, the use of inscribed stones to mark an individual's final resting place.

Pre-Roman British Iron Age burial and funerary practices have been considered as somewhat elusive. Much of ritual practice is not preserved in the archaeological record, and indeed, as Harding notes in his excellent study of death and burial in Iron Age Britain, a persistent misconception is that earlier societies must have buried their dead in a regular and recurrent manner. Thus, when we find no recognisable funerary or burial convention, we view it as a lack or absence when, in reality, it only indicates a plurality of ways in which one community might deal with their dead.[5] In practice, the grave deposition represents only one small stage of a much larger process.

The Celts did not see the world of the living and that of the dead as entirely separated.[6] Instead of physically distancing themselves from the remains of the dead, some of these earlier communities distributed remains – either wholly or in part – around them in what may have been an act of protection or integration.[7] Some made use of exposure (excarnation) or temporary inhumation before a final burial, by which time there may have been only fragmentary remains left. And some made use of dedicated burial spaces – cemeteries – either within a specific area or inside the settlement itself. In the early Iron Age, inhumation was typical for formal burials but later in the period, cremation once again became popular. Some sites even preserve the two methods of disposal together, with cremated remains of one person deposited with the inhumation of another.[8] With such a wide variety of methods and practices surrounding even just the treatment of the corpse, Roman legislation around burial must have seemed excessively restrictive by comparison. In terms of commemorating the dead, common visual markers used by the Celts included stone tombs, cairns (artificially gathered piles of stones) and burial mounds (*tumuli*). There was no tradition of inscribed tombstones until the arrival of the Romans and their epigraphic habit;

indeed, as we will see in some of the examples collected in this book, there were many people in Britannia with Celtic backgrounds who nonetheless chose to be commemorated in this explicitly Roman way.

*   *   *

This book gathers a selection of surviving tombstones across Britannia, from Londinium in the south up to – and even far beyond – the famous frontier of Hadrian's Wall. It is not intended as an in-depth history of the province or the Roman Empire more broadly, and indeed, there are already many excellent books that are well worth consulting if you are interested in finding out more about this historical period. Rather, this collection of ancient stones is intended to provide a snapshot into life in Roman Britain for men, women and children, for the slaves and the freed, and, of course, for the many soldiers who found themselves stationed here. It is an opportunity to meet some of the real people who called the empire's northernmost province their home.

The book also introduces the common Latin conventions that you will encounter on a tombstone and provides guidance on how to read and translate them. For each monument, the epitaph as it appears on the stone (often heavily abbreviated) and the expanded Latin text are provided, along with an English translation. Roman tombstones were, for the most part, highly formulaic. The abbreviations that appear on the tombstones described in this book were used across the empire and form a shared epigraphic vocabulary. Most Roman tombstones from Britannia are written in Latin, the language of the Romans, but a few notable exceptions – such as Ancient Greek and Palmyrene – are included.

In addition to the common modes of expression, there was also a general pattern of information that a Roman epitaph usually recorded. This consisted of the name of the deceased (including their filiation, i.e. their father's name), their voting tribe or nationality, their age at the time of death, and a note on who had set up the monument. Across the empire, many tombstones included a dedication to the spirits of the dead at the very beginning (*Dis Manibus*, abbreviated to D M), which often appeared separate to the rest of the inscription, both visually and grammatically. This dedication acted as a 'genre marker' on the stone, allowing even those who may not have been fully literate to recognise the stone's function.[9] In the case of soldiers, for whom of course we find many memorials in and around Britannia, the epitaph might also include information on their military rank and unit as well as their length of service.

Armed with the knowledge of a handful of commonly found abbreviations, anyone can tackle a bit of decoding. There is something special about being able to connect with words of nearly 2,000 years ago, especially when they mark someone's final resting place. I would encourage anyone to trek to their local museum or Roman fort and have a go at discovering these long-forgotten lives for themselves. A list of common abbreviations can be found at the back of the book for easy reference.

It is worth noting that this little book by no means contains all the hundreds of tombstones recovered so far from Britannia, but it is hoped the small selection gathered here will be enough to encourage you to seek out and appreciate many more of these ancient stories on stone.

Chapter 1

Soldiers

The majority of surviving tombstones from Roman Britain are linked with the army. This is not surprising given the number of soldiers stationed in the province at any one time. Britannia was unusual among the Romans' provincial territories for its strong military presence. The invasion of AD 43 had initially brought four legions to the island: the Second Legion Augusta, the Ninth Legion Hispana, the Fourteenth Legion Gemina and the Twentieth Legion Valeria Victrix. Over time, the specific units changed – the Fourteenth Legion was soon replaced by the Second Legion Adiutrix, the Sixth Legion Victrix was sent to quell a rebellion, the depleted Ninth Legion eventually vanished from records – but for most of its occupation Britannia remained home to three legions of roughly 6,000 men each. The legions were further bolstered by the auxiliary forces: these were military units of non-citizen soldiers from the many territories the Romans had conquered. Auxiliaries were organised into infantry cohorts or cavalry 'wings' (*alae*), which each numbered about 500 men. Yet the high number of units deployed to Britannia – almost seventy by the middle of the second century AD – meant that auxiliary troops outnumbered the legionary contingent.[1] We will encounter many men from these units, in both this chapter and the one that follows, whose tombstones offer us a brief glimpse into military life across the ranks of the vast Roman army.

It is worth noting that individual tombstones were erected to soldiers who died while serving in the army, but this usually did not include those who had died in battle. The logistics of dealing with the dead after a violent clash were obviously very different to dealing with the death of an individual back at the fort, and the Romans did not practise the kind of communal expression of military loss and sacrifice with which we in the modern world are familiar; the idea of a sprawling war cemetery with individual grave markers to memorialise a battlefield, for example, would have been entirely alien.[2] Conquests and victories were celebrated, not the ordinary soldiers who sacrificed their lives out on the battlefield to acquire them. After the end of a battle, the bodies of the dead would be gathered for cremation and then interred there in an unmarked mass grave. As Hope notes, disposal of the war dead was likely 'rapid and unceremonious' as a matter of practicality.[3] In contrast, the cemeteries that were established beside military forts all across the province show the different ways in which an individual soldier could be commemorated when he passed away outside of the battlefield – perhaps succumbing to illness, previous injuries, misfortunate accident or even, as one tombstone attests, killed by a sudden enemy incursion at the camp.[4]

The army did not cover the cost of soldiers' funerary care: their funerals and tombstones were privately funded. Many soldiers belonged to a burial club into which they paid a regular fixed sum that would cover this expense when the time came. As we will see in the selections that follow, some of these monuments were then erected by the heirs the soldiers had nominated in their will – likely their comrades – while others were set up by the families they had suddenly left behind.

AUXILIARY SOLDIERS

CINTUSMUS
FOURTH COHORT OF GAULS

An impressive 'Rotherham red' sandstone memorial featuring a full-body portrait of the deceased survives from the site of Templeborough fort in South Yorkshire.[5] It was recovered during rescue excavations carried out in 1916, at the height of the First World War, when the site was needed for the construction of a steelworks. The tombstone had been broken into two pieces during the Roman period. The larger upper half, which features the depiction of the soldier, had later been reused in a drain at the fort. The lower half, which retains the full inscription set within a panel, was found lining one of the fort's gutters. Although the sandstone is now fairly worn, the depiction of the soldier retains a good amount of detail, and the accompanying inscription remains legible.

<table>
<tr><td>Inscription</td><td>Expanded Text</td></tr>
<tr><td>DIS M CINTVSM</td><td>Dis Manibus Cintusmus</td></tr>
<tr><td>VS M COH IIII GALL</td><td>miles cohortis IIII Gallorum</td></tr>
<tr><td>ORVM PO MELISVS</td><td>posuit Melisus</td></tr>
</table>

Translation
TO THE SPIRITS OF THE DEAD
Cintusmus
soldier in the Fourth Cohort of Gauls
Melisus set this up

The first line contains the standard funerary invocation to the Manes, the spirits of the dead, here written as DIS M. This stands for the phrase *Dis Manibus*, which will be a common fixture on many of the tombstones explored in this book. It usually appears on the first line of an epitaph and is most often found on a separate line to the rest of the inscription. Here, the stonemason has continued to add letters on the same line. This could be a practical choice given the limited space within the panel of the inscription; the mixed sizes of lettering and their slightly haphazard execution suggest a less experienced stonemason.

Following the invocation, we are told the name of the deceased. This is unabbreviated and runs over the first into the second line: Cintusmus (CINTVSMVS). We are only given a single name as identification. This is especially common for Celtic personal names, which we certainly have here. That is not to say it is a particularly unusual or unique name; indeed, we find the name Cintusmus appearing on several other objects including a bronze plaque from Camulodunum (Colchester) that had been dedicated by one 'Cintusmus the coppersmith', as well as decorated bowls signed and stamped by another Cintusmus, this time a potter.[6]

Next on the tombstone's inscription, we are given information about the unit to which Cintusmus belongs as a soldier (*miles*). He is from the Fourth Cohort of Gauls (COH IIII GALLORVM), a part-mounted auxiliary unit that was originally raised in the Roman province of Gallia Lugdunensis in modern-day France – which explains his Celtic/Gallic name. Records place this unit in the province of Moesia in the late first to early second centuries AD, where it was likely involved in the emperor Trajan's wars against the Dacians. The unit was transferred to Britannia at some point before AD 122 and inscriptions locate it in Templeborough early on, then Habitancum (Risingham), then Castlehill fort on the Antonine Wall, before it was then finally stationed at Vindolanda from the early third century AD.

We are not given an age for Cintusmus at the time of his passing, nor are we told how many years he spent in service to the army. The final line of the inscription records that his heir erected the tombstone (PO = *posuit*, the Latin word for 'he/she set up') and his name is written in full as Melisus. As heir, Melisus was responsible for organising the burial of Cintusmus and commissioning the tombstone. This is a useful detail to have on the stone because it tells us that Cintusmus did not die in battle, as burial of soldiers who died on the battlefield was managed and paid for by the military authorities rather than private individuals.[7]

Cintusmus' tombstone may have a brief inscription, but it is accompanied by a magnificent depiction of a standing soldier. This was likely not modelled specifically on Cintusmus himself but chosen as the best way to represent him, showing him as he was during life and emphasising his military career. The monument as a whole measures just under 2 metres tall, and is in two pieces: a large fracture completely separated the lower section of the stone, from the feet of the soldier down. A chunk of stone is also missing from the upper right, beside the figure's neck and shoulder. The figure representing Cintusmus takes up roughly two thirds of the entire monument, while the small panel (roughly 0.1 metres in height by comparison) is positioned beneath his feet. He stands within a recessed shell niche, directly facing

Fig. 1.1 Tombstone of Cintusmus, on display at Clifton Park Museum in Rotherham.

the viewer. Little detail of his features remains beyond his hair, which is cropped close around the top of his head.

Cintusmus is well dressed for life in the northern stretches of Britannia as he wears a thick long cloak called a *paenula*. This type of cloak was usually made from one large section of fabric (coarse wool or felt, sometimes even leather) and fitted over the head. It was ideal for keeping warm and dry when travelling, especially in colder climates, and you can see on this example that Cintusmus' cloak has additional material gathered thickly around his neck – almost like a roll-neck jumper – to keep him warm. He holds the cloak closed at the front with his right hand, and it falls in two long triangular folds past his knees. Underneath the cloak, he wears a tunic, and his lower legs are protected with greaves. A large sword hangs from his belt and in his left hand he clutches a rolled-up scroll, which symbolises his will.

The tombstone provides a striking if sombre image of the soldier whose life is cut short during his service, especially if we imagine it as it stood in its original location outside the fort at Templeborough. Interment took place outside of forts and settlements, in cemeteries that lined the roadsides. Here, in Britannia, far from his native Gaul, Cintusmus would have stood, long after his comrades had departed – at least, until he was recycled for the fort's drainage structures.

DAGVALDA
COHORT OF PANNONIANS

Many tombstones do not survive in their original form, having been deliberately broken up or reshaped for reuse. This is the case with an unusual circular fragment of a Roman tombstone, discovered at Milecastle 42 on Hadrian's Wall.[8] Milecastles were small fort sites placed at intervals of roughly 1 Roman mile along a frontier. Along Hadrian's Wall, there were eighty milecastles in total, each with a gateway through the wall itself. The soldiers garrisoned here – thought to be between ten and thirty at any one time – were responsible for monitoring these frontier gateways, overseeing both military and civilian access to and from the province of Britannia. Milecastle 42 (also known as Cawfields) occupies a strategic position on steep sloping ground overlooking Hole Gap. During excavations in the mid-nineteenth century, this fragment of sepulchral stone was recovered from within the walls of the milecastle. It was considered to have been brought from the cemetery at the nearby Aesica (Great Chesters) fort and reused as a hearthstone.[9] Despite the reshaping of the stone, the majority of the inscription is still visible.

Inscription	**Expanded Text**
D M	*Dis Manibus*
DAGVALDA M[...]	*Dagvalda m[iles cohortis?]*
PAN VIXIT AN[...]	*Pannoniorum vixit an[nos]*
PVSINNA [...]	*Pusinna [coniux]*
[...] X TITVLV[M]	*titulum posuit*

Translation
TO THE SPIRITS OF THE DEAD
Dagvalda soldier in the ? Cohort of
Pannonians lived [...] years
Pusinna his wife
set up this memorial

The inscription just about retains the lower lines of the letters D M, the abbreviated form of the invocation *Dis Manibus*. The letters are placed above the rest of the inscription, carved in a slightly larger size, and well balanced across the space. A line – possibly part of a larger panel – separates the rest of the inscription, which runs over four lines. It is neatly arranged, and the stonemason has used small circular interpuncts to mark spaces between words.

The name of the deceased is given in full at the beginning of the lower inscription block as Dagvalda. The final A is placed inside the D – this could be a deliberate stylistic choice or perhaps a corrected mistake. Dagvalda is an interesting name – and evidently not Roman in origin. It contains a mix of Celtic and Germanic roots: *dag*, from the Celtic for 'good', and *valda*, from the Germanic for 'ruler'.[10] Only a single name is given to identify him, in keeping with Celtic/Germanic naming customs.

Despite the damage, the inscription preserves enough information to surmise some information about the unit to which Dagvalda belonged. He is from a cohort of Pannonians, units originally drawn from the province of Pannonia, but without the numeral, it is difficult to know which cohort precisely. Most readings opt for I as the missing numeral, meaning that Dagvalda belonged to the First Cohort of Pannonians. This would be the only surviving inscription from the province to place this unit – or a small contingent of it – up along Hadrian's Wall. Indeed, the only other evidence for the unit's presence in Britannia at all is a career record from Aesernia for a man called Publius Septimius Paterculus, who is noted as a prefect of the First Cohort of Pannonians in Britannia.[11] As Birley highlights, Dagvalda's tombstone could also have originally read II (Second) or even V (Fifth) Cohort.[12] These two units are more well attested in Britannia – especially in the north, with inscriptions placing men from these units at Bibra (Beckfoot) and Verterae (Brough-under-Stainmore) forts, both in modern-day Cumbria, as well as over towards the eastern end of Hadrian's Wall at Vindolanda – not far from Milecastle 42.

Dagvalda's age was originally given on the tombstone but the numerals after the words *vixit annos* are now missing. It does not look like the number of years' service in the army has been recorded. Instead, the final two lines tell us who set up the monument: his wife Pusinna. This is a more commonly found name than Dagvalda and appears across the Roman Empire, including as a cognomen in the case of Caecina Glyce Pusinna on an inscription from Leptis Magna in modern-day Libya. Here, Pusinna is identified as Dagvalda's wife and the person responsible for setting up the memorial. Although Roman soldiers could not legally marry during their service before AD 197, many nonetheless had *de facto* wives with whom they raised children. A tombstone was not a binding legal document, so Pusinna would have been free to represent herself as Dagvalda's *coniux* ('wife') even if not legally recognised as such.

DECIMUS JULIUS CANDIDUS
FIRST COHORT OF VANGIONES

At Condercum (Benwell), a fort on the eastern side of Hadrian's Wall, archaeologists discovered a tombstone measuring 0.5 metres wide and just over 0.7 metres tall. Like Cintusmus' tombstone, this one had also been recycled in a later Roman building on the same site.[13] Although worn, the original inscription on the sandstone monument can still be read.

Inscription
D M S D IVLIV
S Q F CANDIDVS CHO
P VANGIONVM A XXXX

Expanded Text
Dis Manibus sacrum Decimus Julius
Quinti filius Candidus cohortis
primae Vangionum annorum XXXX

Translation
SACRED TO THE SPIRITS OF THE DEAD
Decimus Julius Candidus, son of Quintus
from the First Cohort of Vangiones
40 years old

The first line begins with a series of letters: the first three (D M S) are to be read together, and form the standard abbreviation for the funerary invocation *Dis Manibus sacrum*, meaning 'sacred to the spirits of the dead'. This is another variation of the formula we will see on the majority of our tombstones; often the word *sacrum* is omitted, and either D M or the full unabbreviated *Dis Manibus* appears instead. This invocation usually appears on the first line of an inscription by itself, but here the stonemason has continued to add letters on the same line. The lack of formal spacing and arrangement suggests either a less experienced stonemason or a lower budget for the creation of this small memorial.

After the invocation is the name of the deceased. This runs over the first line and into the majority of the second: D IVLIVS Q F CANDIDUS. The format follows the general rules around the presentation of names in inscriptions: we are given the praenomen (abbreviated), nomen, then the filiation, and finally the cognomen. The letter D stands for the name Decimus. This is the deceased's praenomen. We are then told that his nomen is Julius (IVLIVS – remember that the Romans do not use the letter J or U). Next, we are given the name of his father through the filiation, which states he is the son (F = *filius*) of Q, the abbreviation for the name Quintus. Finally, we have his cognomen, written in full as Candidus. Piecing these words back together, we can read that the tombstone is therefore for a man called Decimus Julius Candidus, son of Quintus. Three formal names in this manner suggest the deceased was a Roman citizen at the time of his death, and he certainly has a highly Latinised name – as does his father, Quintus. Adopting the Roman cognomen in particular was seemingly common among the Vangiones, and so a more typical Gallo-Germanic name such as Candida became Candidus or Candidius.[14]

Following his identification is the record of the unit to which he belonged within the army. For Candidus, this is the First Cohort (CHO P) of Vangiones (VANGIONVM). This part-mounted auxiliary unit was comprised of men from the Vangiones, a people whose territory lay west of the Rhine. The first record of the cohort is from a diploma of AD 103, though its appearance in a fragmentary legal document recovered in Londinium (London) and dated to AD 67 suggests the unit may have been one of the eight cohorts that were moved to the province from Germany in AD 61.[15] In Britannia, the First Cohort of Vangiones seems to have spent the majority of time stationed in the north, including this site in Condercum as well as Habitancum.

Candidus passed away when he was 40 years old (A = *annorum* plus the numerals XXXX). We are not told how many years he had spent in service to the army by this point, nor are we told who had erected the stone in his memory.

NECTOVELIUS
SECOND COHORT OF THRACIANS

A buff sandstone fragment recovered near the fort of Mumrills in Stirlingshire preserves a full panel inscription from a tombstone that gives us more information about the recruitment of men into different auxiliary units. The fragment itself measures just under 0.5 metres wide and about 0.33 metres tall. Despite some damage, it fortunately still captures all six lines of the inscribed epitaph. The letters still showed traces of red paint when discovered.

Inscription
DIS M NECTOVELIVS F
VINDICIS AN IXXX
STIP VIIII NAT
IONIS BRIGANS
MILITAVIT IN
COH II THR

Expanded Text
Dis Manibus Nectovelius filius
Vindicis annorum IXXX
stipendiorum VIIII
nationis Brigans
militavit in
cohorte II Thracum

Translation
TO THE SPIRITS OF THE DEAD
Nectovelius son of Vindex
29 years old
with 9 years' service
from the Brigantes people
served in
the Second Cohort of Thracians

The inscription on this tombstone begins with the standard invocation to the Manes, though written in a slightly rarer formula this time – DIS M – which combines the full first word with the abbreviation for the second. This is not kept to its own line but followed immediately by the name of the deceased: Nectovelius. This is another striking Celtic name, as is the name of his father, which is provided afterwards in the filiation son of Vindex (F VINDICIS).

The second and third lines provide information on Nectovelius' age and the amount of time he had spent in the army. We are told that he passed away at the age of 29 (IXXX = 9 and 20), after having completed nine (VIIII) years of military service.

Most interestingly, perhaps, the tombstone records Nectovelius' nationality as well as the unit to which he belonged within the Roman auxiliary forces. And it is perhaps a surprising contrast, for Nectovelius is a local boy from Britannia – from the Brigantes people, to be precise. The Brigantes were a federation of tribes who controlled the largest expanse of territory in ancient Britain, which stretched across the north of modern-day England. Following the establishment of Britannia as a Roman province, the Brigantes were reorganised into a *civitas*. Nectovelius identifies himself as a native of the Brigantes people, and so he is not especially far from home even up at the fort of Mumrills. The final lines tell us about the unit he joined: the Second Cohort of Thracians. This part-mounted auxiliary unit was originally recruited from the Thracian territories incorporated into the province of Thracia by the Romans. But this tombstone tells us that the unit later recruited from the native populations around where it was stationed.

LEGIONARY SOLDIERS

JULIUS JULIANUS
SECOND LEGION AUGUSTA

Around 3 miles from the site of Isca Silurum (Caerleon) fort in modern-day South Wales, the tombstone of a legionary soldier was rediscovered by chance at St Andrew's Church in Tredunnock.[16] During the 1670s, the sexton had been digging out the ground to prepare a grave when he noticed the stone, which had been fastened with iron pins to the ground wall of the church. A record of its discovery along with a sketch of the stone appears in Camden's 1695 *Britannia*, where the author puzzles over its location:

> Considering this is the monument of a heathen, and must be about fourteen or fifteen hundred years standing; it seems strange it should be reposited in this place, and thus fastened to the foundation of the church: unless we suppose it laid there by some pious Christian in after ages, or rather that the church was built on some burial place.[17]

The church itself is thought to have been built in the twelfth and thirteenth centuries, and even then, it would not have been unusual for ancient Roman stones to be recycled for construction – even if they were indeed 'heathen' tombstones. After its discovery, the tombstone was removed and placed inside the church, where it is still on display today. The funerary monument is carved from reddish sandstone, roughly 1 metre wide and 0.7 metres tall. The inscription is placed at the centre within an ansate style frame and runs over seven lines. The letters are neat and uniform, and the stonemason has made use of small triangular interpuncts. Fortunately, the epitaph has not suffered any damage and remains very clear.

<table>
<tr><td align="center">Inscription</td><td align="center">Expanded Text</td></tr>
<tr><td align="center">D M IVL IVLIANUS</td><td align="center">Dis Manibus Julius Julianus</td></tr>
<tr><td align="center">MIL LEG II AVG STIP</td><td align="center">miles legionis II Augustae stipendiorum</td></tr>
<tr><td align="center">XVIII ANNOR XL</td><td align="center">XVIII annorum XL</td></tr>
<tr><td align="center">HIC SITVS EST</td><td align="center">hic situs est</td></tr>
<tr><td align="center">CVRA AGENTE</td><td align="center">curam agente</td></tr>
<tr><td align="center">AMANDA</td><td align="center">Amanda</td></tr>
<tr><td align="center">CONIVGE</td><td align="center">coniuge</td></tr>
</table>

Translation
TO THE SPIRITS OF THE DEAD
Julius Julianus
soldier in the Second Legion Augusta
with 18 years' service, 40 years old
HERE HE LIES
Amanda his wife
took care of this

The inscription opens with our expected invocation, here abbreviated fully to D M (*Dis Manibus*). Immediately following this, on the same line, we find the name of the deceased, Julius Julianus. The second line provides information on his role and unit, describing him explicitly as *miles* (MIL), a soldier, and identifying him as belonging to the Second Legion Augusta (LEG II AVG). This legion was raised in the latter years of the Roman Republic and spent time in Hispania, Germania and Gaul before heading to Britannia to support Claudius' invasion in AD 43 under the command of Aulus Plautius. It was originally stationed in the south, moving from Silchester to Dorchester, then to Isca Dumnoniorum (Exeter), and on to Gloucester. In AD 75, the legion was then moved to Isca Silurum, where it remained for the majority of its time in Britannia. We know from building stones that the Second Legion was mobile and it – or a contingent from it – headed far enough north to support the building of Hadrian's Wall as well as the Antonine Wall in the second century AD. During Septimius Severus' attempts to conquer the tribes beyond Hadrian's Wall in AD 208, the legion was briefly stationed at Carpow with the Sixth Legion, before once again returning to Isca Silurum.

Unlike many of the auxiliary soldiers' tombstones, we are not given any information on where Julius Julianus himself hailed from in the Roman Empire. Legionaries were originally primarily recruited from Italy but as the empire expanded, and their citizen base grew, this naturally changed: by the end of the first century AD, legionary recruits came from a range of provinces including Germania, Hispania, Gallia and North Africa.[18] We do know that Julianus had served a lengthy stretch in the army by the time of his death: the third line of the inscription tells us that he had completed eighteen years of service. We are then given his age at the time of death as 40. This means Julianus had joined the army at the age of 22, slightly older than the majority of recruits who typically enlisted between the ages of 17 and 20.[19] He was by no means an old recruit, though, as the army did allow men to join up to the age of 35.

On the fourth line of the tombstone we find another popular phrase from epitaphs, here wholly unabbreviated: HIC SITVS EST. This is best translated as 'here he lies', a sentiment that is not unfamiliar to modern epitaphs, too. On the many Roman tombstones across Britannia, this phrase usually appears in its abbreviated form (HSE) – indeed, only one other example survives in which it is written out in full (RIB932). Usually, the abbreviation appears at the end of the inscription, but here on Julianus' tombstone three more lines follow. These identify who has set up the memorial: a woman called Amanda, who is clearly identified as Julianus' wife (*coniuge*). As we have seen already with the tombstone of the auxiliary soldier Dagvalda, soldiers often had *de facto* wives who would not legally have been recognised as such before AD 197 – but that would not have prevented Amanda from identifying as Julianus' wife on his tombstone. The *de facto* arrangement seems likely to be the case here, as the tombstone has been considered 'undoubtedly' second century – likely Antonine – based on its lettering style, with some suggesting it may well be the earliest example from the province of a serving soldier's wife being named on his memorial stone.[20]

TITUS VALERIUS PUDENS
SECOND LEGION ADIUTRIX PIA FIDELIS

During excavations at Monson Street in Lincoln in 1849, broken pieces of a tombstone were found buried in an almost 2.5-metre-deep hole along with other Roman artefacts.[21] This area falls within the site of a Roman cemetery, and several other tombstones as well as buried and cremated human remains have been recovered there. During the Roman occupation, Lindum (Lincoln) was initially established as a legionary fortress. Towards the end of the first century AD, it became a *colonia* – this was a high-ranking chartered town that, in the Roman provinces, was created through land grants for legionary veterans. This cemetery site lay to the south of the settlement, by the roadside. Remains of the Fosse Way can still be seen under the twelfth-century St Mary's Guildhall, which sits just around the corner from modern-day Monson Street.

Excavation coverage from the time noted that this tombstone looked to have been deliberately broken up into pieces and then buried. Fortunately, this meant that although the stone had been damaged, the fragments themselves had not been scattered or reused. Reconstructed, the monument measures around 1.8 metres tall by just over 0.5 metres wide. It features a gabled panel with inscription, plus further carved imagery below the panel itself. Despite some large cracks running through the inscription, the lettering remains almost entirely legible.

Inscription	Expanded Text
T VALERIVS T F	*Titus Valerius Titi filius*
CLA PVDENS SAV	*Claudia Pudens Savaria*
MIL LEG II A P F	*miles legionis II Adiutricis Piae Fidelis*
DOSSENNI	*Dossenni*
PROCVLI A XXX	*Proculi annorum XXX*
AERA [V] I H D S P	*aera [V] I heres de suo posuit*
H S E	*hic situs est*

Translation
Titus Valerius Pudens, son of Titus
of the Claudian voting tribe, from Savaria
soldier in the Second Legion Adiutrix Pia Fidelis
in the century of Dossennius Proculus
30 years old with 6 years' service
his heir set this up with his own money
HERE HE LIES

The tombstone is dedicated to a man called Titus Valerius Pudens. His naming here across the first two lines follows the conventional arrangement by providing his praenomen (T) and nomen (VALERIVS), then his filiation (T F) and voting tribe (CLA), and then his cognomen (PVDENS). From this, we already know that the deceased's father was also named Titus, and that he belonged to the Claudian voting tribe. Here we are also told that he was originally from Savaria – modern-day Szombathely in Hungary. Savaria was itself a *colonia*, which had been established in Pannonia Superior by the emperor Claudius. Noticeably missing from this inscription is the standard opening invocation to the spirits of the dead, either abbreviated or unabbreviated, suggesting that this tombstone was erected at an early date.

Next, we are given information about Pudens' military career: he was a soldier in the Second Legion Adiutrix Pia Fidelis (LEG II A P F) and belonged to the century of a man called Dossennius Proculus. During the imperial period, a century was a military unit of eighty soldiers under the command of a centurion. The Second Legion Adiutrix was established in AD 70 by the emperor Vespasian. Its title Adiutrix comes from the Latin for 'helper' (similar to the modern term 'adjutant') and is sometimes referred to as the 'Rescuer' legion. Much of this legion was originally comprised of men from the Imperial Navy's Ravenna fleet who had proven faithful to Vespasian during his challenge to Vitellius' brief imperial rule in AD 69, hence their honorary title Pia Fidelis – 'pious and faithful'. The legion was first sent to Germania Inferior under the general Quintus Petillius Cerialis to help quell the Batavian revolt alongside other legionary forces in AD 70. The following year it was sent to Britannia – again with Cerialis – to help against the rebellion of the Brigantes. Evidence places the legion at Lindum for several years until about AD 77 before it then moved to Deva Victrix (Chester) though it was often deployed to support forces fighting against the tribes to the west and to the north. It remained in Britannia until AD 87. This provides an initial window of time for Pudens' tombstone to have been erected in Lindum's cemetery between AD 71 and 77.

Across the fifth and sixth lines we are told that Pudens' age at the time of death was 30 (XXX) and by this point he had served in the unit for six years (AERA VI). The numeral V is missing on the stone but is the most likely reconstruction: older line drawings and photographs of the stone show it with slightly more lettering and indentations surviving around the damage than is currently there now. Given Pudens had served in the legion for six years, then it is possible his death occurred in AD 76 – i.e. six years after the legion was created in AD 70. The legion was stationed in Lindum at this point.

The epitaph ends with two abbreviated phrases. The first (HDSP = *heres de suo posuit*) declares that Pudens' heir (*heres*) had set up the monument (*posuit*) at their own expense (*de suo*). We are not given the name of the heir who has taken on this task, though it is possible in this case it would have been one of his comrades in the army. Perhaps Pudens had not yet deposited enough in his burial club account to cover his funeral costs. He had only served six years in the legion, after all.

The inscription closes with the abbreviated phrase *hic situs est* (HSE), 'here he lies', reminding us of the original link between this stone and Pudens' mortal remains. The tombstone design is simple but striking: within a carved gabled border are two dolphins swimming downwards towards a central trident. This clear nautical imagery – dolphins and the trident both symbols of Neptune, the Roman god of the sea – certainly supports the idea that Pudens was recruited from the Imperial Navy. Carved beneath the inscription panel is an axe known as a *dolabra*: this was not a weapon but a tool often used by the legionary soldiers for digging.

LUCIUS BEBIUS CRESCENS
SIXTH LEGION

During the construction of a new gymnasium at The Mount School in York in 1911, a tombstone was discovered nearly 3 metres below the ground.[22] It was buried face-upwards and had narrowly escaped being covered by the foundation of a wall that had been erected in 1855. This south-westerly area of Roman Eboracum (modern-day York) was the site of a cemetery, which, based on the elaborate stonework and varied grave goods recovered, must have been a large and important site.

This particular tombstone recovered from The Mount School site had survived in very good condition. It measures just under 2 metres tall by 0.7 metres wide. It is of fairly plain decoration: the gabled top features a rosette within the recessed pediment. The majority of the stone is occupied by the inscription, neatly cut over nine lines and set within a recessed panel.

<table>
<tr><td align="center">Inscription</td><td align="center">Expanded Text</td></tr>
<tr><td align="center">D M</td><td align="center">Dis Manibus</td></tr>
<tr><td align="center">L BEBVS</td><td align="center">Lucius Bebius</td></tr>
<tr><td align="center">AVG CRES</td><td align="center">Augusta Crescens</td></tr>
<tr><td align="center">CENS VN</td><td align="center">Vindelicum</td></tr>
<tr><td align="center">ML LEG VI</td><td align="center">miles legionis VI</td></tr>
<tr><td align="center">VIC P F</td><td align="center">Victricis Piae Fidelis</td></tr>
<tr><td align="center">AN XLIII</td><td align="center">annorum XLIII</td></tr>
<tr><td align="center">STP XXIII</td><td align="center">stipendiorum XXIII</td></tr>
<tr><td align="center">H A F C</td><td align="center">heres amico faciendum curavit</td></tr>
</table>

Translation

TO THE SPIRITS OF THE DEAD
Lucius Bebius Crescens
from Augusta Vindelicum
soldier in the Sixth Legion
Victrix Pia Fidelis
43 years old
with 23 years' service
his heir took care to set this up for his friend

The inscription features several ligatures: this means that the stonemason has combined some letters together rather than cut them separately. This can be seen in the inscription's second line, where the letterform I has been combined with the vertical side stroke of the second B, hence the name being transcribed above as Bebius not Bebus. The mason has made similar combinations later in the inscription for IN, IL and IP.

After the standard funerary invocation *Dis Manibus*, here abbreviated fully as D M, the epitaph records the *tria nomina* of the deceased, Lucius Bebius Crescens. The praenomen is indicated only by the letter L, while the other names are here written in full. Crescens is identified as hailing from Augusta Vindelicum (modern-day Augsburg in Germany), a large Roman settlement established initially as a legionary camp in the territory of the Gallic Vindelici. Over time, as the camp fell out of use, the civilian settlement expanded and Augusta Vindelicum later became the provincial capital of Raetia.

Crescens is identified as a soldier with the Sixth Legion Victrix. On the inscription, a line has been added over VI in the fifth line to indicate this is a number rather than a word. This is a common epigraphic habit, and especially useful in this case to differentiate the numeral from one of the legion's honorary titles, *Victrix*, here abbreviated to VIC but often appearing as simply VI on other inscriptions. The Sixth Legion bears three titles: *Victrix Pia Fidelis* (VIC P F), which can be translated as 'Victorious, Loyal and Faithful'. The Sixth Legion Victrix was originally established by Octavian (later to become the emperor Augustus) in 41 BC, using veterans from Caesar's own Sixth Legion. It was first deployed in Italy and Sicily, and then later took part in the famous Battle of Actium against Mark Antony and Cleopatra in 31 BC. During the expansion of the Roman Empire, the legion was sent to Hispania, where it was stationed for several decades, then Germania Inferior, before being sent by the emperor Hadrian to the north of Britannia in or just before AD 122. While there, the legion was based at Eboracum, though the soldiers often spent time further north, supporting major building works including the construction of Hadrian's Wall and the Antonine Wall. Given Crescens' burial at the cemetery in Eboracum, he must have died while the legion was back at its base.

We are told on the tombstone that Crescens was 43 when he passed away. By this point, he had served for a total of twenty-three years in the army, having enlisted at the age of 20, and therefore was close to reaching the twenty-five- or twenty-six-year point of retirement. The final line explains that his heir (*heres*) set up the monument for his friend, though yet again the heir's name is not recorded on the inscription itself.

LUCIUS SEMPRONIUS FLAVINUS
NINTH LEGION

A fragmented tombstone found in Lindum records the death of a soldier from the Ninth Legion, a unit whose mysterious disappearance from records has captured the modern imagination.[23] The stone itself had been later reused in the foundations of a Roman wall, and was rediscovered in 1830 during the building of new houses on the Lindum Road. The gabled grave marker has been badly damaged through the years: the lower part is now lost and the surface is heavily worn. The remaining fragment measures 1.3 metres tall and just under 1 metre wide. The central gable point is flanked by two smaller acroteria; all three feature an incised rosette pattern.

The inscription is set within a bordered panel, though the lower border is lost along with the rest of the stone. Within the panel, the inscribed letters are still visible. The rather unusual cursive writing style led to some confusion over the words when first discovered.

<table>
<tr><td align="center">Inscription</td><td align="center">Expanded Text</td></tr>
<tr><td align="center">L SEMPRONI FLA</td><td align="center">Luci Semproni</td></tr>
<tr><td align="center">VINI MILTS LEG VIIII</td><td align="center">Flavini militis legionis VIIII</td></tr>
<tr><td align="center">BABVDI SEVERI</td><td align="center">Babudi Severi</td></tr>
<tr><td align="center">AER VII ANOR XXX</td><td align="center">aerum VII annorum XXX</td></tr>
<tr><td align="center">ISPANI GALERIA</td><td align="center">Hispani Galeria</td></tr>
<tr><td align="center">CLVNIA</td><td align="center">Clunia</td></tr>
</table>

Translation

For Lucius Sempronius Flavinus
soldier in the Ninth Legion
in the century of Babudius Severus
7 years service, 30 years old
a Spaniard from Clunia, of
the Galerian voting tribe

This tombstone does not feature the invocation to the spirits of the dead but rather begins with the name of the deceased. This suggests an early date within the first century AD before *Dis Manibus* became the prevalent funerary custom. His *tria nomina* is written in the dative case: here, this means that his names in the Latin text end with *-i* rather than the usual *-us*. The dative case appears often on inscriptions, indicating that the monument in question has been erected *to* or *for* a particular person.

Flavinus is identified as a soldier in the Ninth Legion. This legion was also known as *Legio IX Hispana*. It was sent to Britannia early on, from the time of Claudius' invasion in AD 43, and moved across the province over the next several years. They established a legionary fortress at Lindum at some point in the late AD 50s to 60s. The legion suffered a catastrophic defeat during the Boudiccan rebellion in AD 61; after reinforcements from Germania arrived to replenish its numbers, the legion was then involved in campaigns against the Brigantes and by AD 71 it had moved on to Eboracum. Yet by the early second century AD, the legion disappeared from all military records with no explanation. Flavinus' tombstone was thus erected at some point during the legion's occupation of Lindum – so at the very least, a cut-off date of AD 71 for Flavinus' death seems reasonable.

The third line of this tombstone records which century Flavinus belonged to specifically within the Ninth Legion: that of Babudius Severus. Babudius Severus, as the centurion, would have been responsible for training, disciplining and leading his unit. We have no other information about this particular centurion, though Birley notes his 'good Italian name'.[24] The letterforms used in the third line for the name Babudius are especially interesting for their noticeably cursive style; instead of the standard forms found in epigraphy, the letters resemble the handwriting used in other Roman writing – like that on wooden tablets, or even graffiti.

The fourth line notes that Flavinus had served in the army for seven years at the time of his death. He was 30 years old by then, and so must have joined the legion at the slightly older age of 23. The final two lines of the inscription provide information about Flavinus' background. He is originally from the province of Hispania – a point of much pride, given it is emphasised through his description as a Spaniard (*Hispani*) as well as the identification of his home city (Clunia, a prosperous *colonia* in the north) and his voting tribe (Galerian). These three aspects reinforce his identity while also lamenting on how far he now finds himself from his beloved home.

A second tombstone of the same shape and design, also dedicated to a soldier from the Ninth Legion, was found in Lincoln in 1865. This monument to a soldier by the name of Gaius Saufeius survives in much better condition, preserving the full stone and three clear rosettes along with the recessed inscription. The similarity between this and the previous tombstone suggests a vendor who sold pre-made 'blank' monuments for individuals to then later add their required epitaph. The same mason may have made the two tombstones but they certainly did not share the same cutter for the epitaph: the inscription on Saufeius' stone is much more uniformly carved in comparison to Flavinus' unusual cursive-leaning script.

TITUS FLAMINUS
FOURTEENTH LEGION

An intriguing tombstone fragment belonging to a soldier of the Fourteenth Legion was recovered during excavation work at the Roman cemetery to the east of Viroconium (Wroxeter) in 1861.[25] The area later known as Viroconium was occupied early on in the Claudian invasion by auxiliary troops, with the Fourteenth Legion then establishing a fort in the middle of the first century AD. By AD 80, the legion was taken north by Agricola to support his campaigns. The fort was then occupied by the Twentieth Legion for a few years, and after their departure the site grew as a civilian settlement, eventually becoming one of the largest cities in the province.

This sandstone fragment was found buried face-down in the soil and had been badly damaged: the original relief that stood above the inscription was missing, with only the feet of the figure left behind. The inscription panel remained, and though it showed considerable wear to some of the lettering, it was clear that this particular epitaph was unique. It runs across seven lines in total.

Inscription	Expanded Text
[F] LAMINVS T POL FA	*Flaminus Titi Pollia Faventia*
[AN] NORVM XXXXV STIP XXII MIL LEG	*annorum XXXXV stipendiorum XXII miles legionis*
[X] IIII GEM MILITAVI AQ NVNC HIC S[V] M	*XIIII Geminae militavi atque nunc hic sum*
[...] LEGITE ET FELICES VITA PLVS MIN E[...]	*[hoc] legite et felices vita plus minus este*
[D] I VVA VINI ET AQUA PROHIBENT VBI	*di uva vini et aqua prohibent ubi*
TA[R] TAR ADITIS VIVITE DVM SI[...]	*Tartara aditis vivite dum si[dus]*
VITAE DAT TEMPVS HONESTE	*vitae dat tempus honeste*

Translation
Flaminus son of Titus, from the Pollian voting tribe
45 years old with 22 years' service, a soldier in the
14th Legion Gemina. I served as a soldier and now I am here.
Read this and be more or less happy in life!
The gods forbid wine and water when
you arrive in Tartarus. Live well
while fate allows time for life!

The inscription begins as we might expect: we have the name of the deceased stated first (Flaminus) and we are told the name of his father (Titus), followed by a quick succession of basic information about his life and military service. Flaminus belonged to the Pollian voting tribe, one of the older rural tribes, which dated back to the sixth century BC. He was 45 when he passed away, by which point he had completed a long military career of twenty-two years.

We are told that Flaminus belonged to the Fourteenth Legion Gemina (LEG XIII): this legion had its origin during the Roman Republic under Julius Caesar to support his Gallic Wars. It later gained the title Gemina ('twin') after being merged with one of Mark Antony's legions following his defeat at the Battle of Actium in 31 BC. The Fourteenth Legion fought in Germany and Gaul before supporting Claudius' invasion of Britannia in AD 43. It remained in Britannia until AD 67. Initially stationed in Ratae (Leicester), it was deployed around the province to quell uprisings from several different local tribes to the north and west. From AD 55, the legion was stationed at Viroconium. This tells us that Flaminus' death must have therefore occurred between AD 55 and 67.

After the initial two and a half lines of fairly standard military epitaph we then have something very different. The inscription changes midway through the third line from an indirect record of information to an epigram of direct address from the deceased himself. The lines that Flaminus 'speaks' to the passer-by are composed in three hexameters, the metre of the great ancient epic poets like Homer and Virgil. Across the short verse, Flaminus briefly laments his fate before offering some advice to the passer-by.

Flaminus' opening line – 'I served as a soldier and now I am here' – bleakly summarises his life in just five short Latin words, while also literally acknowledging his final physical resting place. The first verb, *militavi* ('I served as a soldier'), uses the perfect tense to indicate an action that is now completed; this contrasts neatly with the final verb of the line, *sum* ('I am'), in the present tense to denote his now continuous state of death. The epitaph also references the very monument on which it is carved through the short word *hic* ('here'), creating an intriguing dialogue between message and object. This initial message also interacts with the information that came before, as we know Flaminus has ended up *here* – in a cemetery of Viroconium far from home – because he spent the majority of his adult life in the army. This was the focus of his life and remains the focus now in death, too.

Flaminus then issues instructions to the reader of his tombstone using two imperatives – 'Read (*legite*) this and be (*este*) more or less happy in life!' An imperative is a direct verbal command, which, in Latin, changes form depending on whether it is addressed to one person (singular) or more than one person (plural). Here we have the plural forms, which tells us that Flaminus did not intend to address a specific person, but rather his message was intended to speak to all who happen to come upon his tombstone. His advice is clear: read his epitaph and find some joy in life, for at least you are not in his unfortunate position.

Over the next two lines, he explains that the gods forbid wine and water when you arrive in Tartarus – i.e. when you are dead. Tartarus was a region in the Graeco-Roman underworld, though the location's name is often used by the ancients as a way of referencing death and the underworld more generally. In early Greek descriptions of the underworld, Tartarus was the deepest and furthest region: the ancient poet Hesiod noted that if you dropped an anvil from the upper world, it would take nine days to reach Tartarus.[26] It became the home of the imprisoned Titans after their defeat by Zeus and the Olympian gods. Over time, Tartarus became a destination for the immoral. Many mythological characters find their eternal punishment there, like Sisyphus, who is destined to push his heavy boulder to the top of a hill, only for it to roll back down as soon as he reaches the top. Regular mortals – such as terrible tyrants or those who have harmed their own families – could also find themselves sent to Tartarus for punishment. Here, rather than reference the specific region, Flaminus seems to be speaking more broadly: the dead can no longer consume wine or water once they have passed into the next life. This is given as a reason for the passer-by to enjoy life while they still can: soon, many regular mortal pleasures will be inaccessible to them. He emphasises this part of his message with one final further command, again using the imperative form to issue forth his order: 'Live (*vivite*) well while fate allows time for life!' Mortals are living a life apportioned to them by Fate – they cannot control the length they have been given, and cannot know when their time will be up. Therefore, they should make the most of it while they still can.

The custom of funerary epitaphs that directly engaged the passer-by with maxims about the brevity of life – and thus the need to enjoy it while you can – had a long tradition stretching back to the Ancient Greeks. Here, on Flaminus' tombstone, the stark contrast between life and death is repeatedly emphasised through this direct address from the dead to the living, which, in its original context – a large monument featuring a likeness of Flaminus himself, standing tall in a roadside cemetery – must have certainly prompted a few passers-by to reflect on their own mortality.

FURIUS MAXIMUS
TWENTIETH LEGION VALERIA VICTRIX

A handful of tombstone fragments from Deva were discovered in 1887 in the city's north wall, where they had been reused as building material.[27] Reassembled, they do not form a full tombstone: the surviving pieces create the right-hand side of a monument that originally consisted of an upper relief with a recessed panel inscription below. The lower right portion of the relief survives with good detail, while the inscription beneath is fully legible.

Inscription	Expanded Text
D M	*Dis Manibus*
FVRI MAXI	*Furi Maxi-*
MI	*-mi*
MIL LEG XX V V	*militis legionis XX Valeriae Victricis*
STI XXII	*stipendiorum XXII*
H F C	*heres faciendum curavit*

Translation
TO THE SPIRITS OF THE DEAD
For Furius Maximus
soldier in the Twentieth Legion Valeria Victrix
of 22 years' service
his heir took care to set this up

The inscription begins with the customary invocation to the Manes, followed by the deceased's name. Here the name is written in the dative case – the two given names over lines two and three ending with *-i* rather than *-us* – to signal the monument's dedication to both the spirits of the dead and the deceased. The deceased is a man called Furius Maximus. The fourth line then tells us that he is a soldier from the Twentieth Legion (*militis legionis* XX), a unit that bore the title 'Valeria Victrix' in Latin. This honorary title can be translated to 'brave and victorious'.

The Twentieth Legion was likely founded during the reign of Augustus, and it was quickly sent to Hispania Tarraconensis to support the Roman campaigns against the Cantabrians (25–19 BC). It then spent time in the provinces of Illyricum and Germania Inferior, before accompanying the emperor Claudius on his initial invasion of Britannia in AD 43. It remained in the province until at least the end of the third century BC and during this time moved around extensively. Evidence initially places the unit at Camulodunum immediately after the invasion, where it constructed the province's first legionary fortress. It was stationed here until AD 49. Next, the legion spent several years in Glevum (Gloucester), until it was eventually sent west to Burrium (Usk) to help fight against the Silures. Although this proved unsuccessful, a few years later the Twentieth Legion was one of several Roman forces that successfully quelled Boudicca's revolt in AD 60/61.

By AD 66, the unit was stationed at Viroconium. It was then sent north to support the campaigns of Agricola between AD 78 and 84, and at one point the legion occupied the far northerly legionary fortress at Inchtuthil in Caledonia. By AD 88, the unit was on the move again – this time, back down to Deva Victrix, which became the legion's home for around 200 years. Although this was their base, it did not mean the soldiers did not continue to move around; the Twentieth Legion was one of the key units involved in the construction of Hadrian's Wall. Furius Maximus' tombstone would thus have been erected at some point in a fairly wide window of time between AD 88 and when the legion departed.

On the tombstone itself, we are not given Furius Maximus' age at the time of his death, but we are told that he had completed twenty-two years of service in the army. This suggests he was likely in his early to mid-forties when he died. His monument has been erected by his heir (H F C = *heres faciendum curavit*), who remains unnamed on the stone, and there are few other details to help narrow down the date much further.

The inscription on this tombstone is perhaps shorter than some of the others we have encountered so far, but I have chosen to include it as it is accompanied by a wonderful fragmentary image of Furius Maximus. Rather than showing him standing in his military attire, the stone instead depicts him in the midst of a dinner party. Only the lower right section of the scene survives but the arrangement is clear: a male figure reclines on a large couch (*lectus*). A couch was a common piece of Roman furniture used for sitting, reclining and sleeping. The individual's weight was supported by a base of crossed leather straps across a wooden frame, which was covered with soft furnishings including pillows and covers on a light mattress. Roman couches are often shown, as here, with a high back and carved legs. Furius Maximus reclines comfortably on the couch, leaning on his left side. He is dressed in a simple tunic, which falls in folds over his body. His right arm is raised and likely once held a cup. A small three-legged (tripod) table is set in front of the couch.

Dinner party scenes like this are often found on Roman tombstones, particularly those from military sites in and around the frontiers. From Deva alone we find several other examples, some of which survive in slightly better overall condition but preserve less information about the deceased themselves. These tombstone fragments were also discovered rebuilt in the same eastern section of the north wall in 1887, and are all dedicated to soldiers, suggesting that they were all originally taken from the same section of an older Roman cemetery.

The second 'dining' tombstone was found in two larger pieces: it had been broken in half across the middle, separating the inscription from the upper relief.[28] Both halves survive in fair condition though some stone around the top and bottom has been lost, and the faces of the figures do not survive. The inscription is set within a panel and spans seven lines, which fortunately have remained intact.

<table>
<tr><td align="center">Inscription</td><td align="center">Expanded Text</td></tr>
<tr><td align="center">D M</td><td align="center">Dis Manibus</td></tr>
<tr><td align="center">CECILIVSDONATVSB</td><td align="center">Cecilius Donatus B-</td></tr>
<tr><td align="center">ESSVSNA</td><td align="center">essus na-</td></tr>
<tr><td align="center">TIONEMILI</td><td align="center">tione mili-</td></tr>
<tr><td align="center">TAVITANN</td><td align="center">tavit ann-</td></tr>
<tr><td align="center">OS XX VIVIV</td><td align="center">os XXVI viv-</td></tr>
<tr><td align="center">ITANNOSXXXX</td><td align="center">it annos XXXX</td></tr>
</table>

Translation
TO THE SPIRITS OF THE DEAD
Cecilius Donatus
a Bessian national
served 26 years in the army
lived 40 years

The lettering is not especially well spaced: some words run together and over lines, while some have unusual breaks between letters, and the third line sits particularly off-centre compared to the rest. This could suggest a stonemason who was not as familiar with the Latin language. We have the customary invocation to the gods at the beginning (D M), but beyond this the composer of this epitaph has chosen to use no other abbreviations – thus we find full Latin verbs, such as *militavit* ('he served in the army') and *vivit* ('he lived'), as well as the full term *annos* ('years').

We are told that this monument was erected for a man called Cecilius Donatus. More typically written as Caecilius, the loss of the diphthong 'ae' in the name suggests either a simple spelling error in the carving process or perhaps a later date for the monument when 'e' began to replace the diphthong. We know that Donatus served in the army and had a considerably lengthy career of twenty-six years. This is interesting when paired with his given age at the time of death – 40 – as it would suggest he enlisted in the army at the young age of 14. Keeping in mind the tendency for rounding up or down to whole numbers on monuments as noted in the introduction, we may interpret this more flexibly as Donatus joining the army in his teens and then passing away in his forties.

We are not told to which unit Donatus belonged, though we are given some information on his background: Donatus is described as originally hailing from the Bessian people who were located in the western region of ancient Thrace. This has led to some suggestions that he perhaps belonged to the Second Legion Adiutrix, whose recruitment, reflecting the men's original entry into the imperial fleet at Ravenna, drew from areas including Thrace. Others have suggested that the lack of praenomen, voting tribe, or father's name recorded as part of the inscription, in addition to his recruitment from the Bessians, indicates a later third-century date and so Donatus must have belonged to the Twentieth Legion.[29] The latter seems more likely in this case. But whatever his unit, it is interesting to note that Donatus' memorialisation combines a highly Romanised self-presentation with this clear acknowledgement of his native roots.

The relief on Donatus' tombstone is better preserved than that of Furius Maximus. Positioned within an arched recess, Donatus reclines on a large high-backed couch. He leans on his left side and in his left hand clutches a scroll, representing his will. His right arm is raised and he holds up a cup in his hand. His civilian attire falls loosely in folds around his body. He is joined at his dinner by a woman – presumably his wife – who is positioned behind him, also reclining on her left side. Neither face survives. In front of the couch is a small three-legged table with an assortment of food items, including a small circular loaf of bread. It is a scene of comfortable relaxation, whether showing the deceased as he once enjoyed life or depicting him in an eternal afterlife banquet.

A third 'dinner party' tombstone recovered from the very same location in Chester's north wall shows a slight variation on the typical dining scene.[30] This monument was also recovered in two sections, having been broken across the middle. It would once have been an imposing monument as the two fragments when taken together measure just over 1.3 metres in their current condition. The upper fragment retains most of a relief depicting the deceased while the lower fragment, although badly damaged, preserves some additional details from the relief's edge along with a short inscription.

Inscription
[D] M
AURELI LUCI
EQVITIS
H F C

Expanded Text
Dis Manibus
Aureli Luci
equitis
heres faciendum curavit

Translation
TO THE SPIRITS OF THE DEAD
For Aurelius Lucius
horseman
his heir took care to set this up

The lettering remains clear and neatly spaced with interpuncts. The epitaph itself provides a snippet of information about the deceased: he was called Aurelius Lucius, he was a horseman, and his heir saw to the erection of the monument after his death. We are not given an age or length of service, nor do we learn to which cavalry unit he belonged. Instead, however, we have a remarkable depiction of the deceased, which blends Roman style with several notably non-Roman details.

As with the two previous examples, Lucius reclines comfortably on a couch, leaning on his left side. The couch here has a lower back than the others, though is equally well furnished with a thick mattress and a supporting cushion. In his left hand he clutches a rolled scroll, symbolising his will. His right arm is raised, bending at the elbow, and he holds up a cup with his right hand. Unlike the others, however, Lucius is not dressed in the clothes of a Roman man at leisure. Instead, he wears loose trousers and a thick long-sleeved top, which sits closely around his neck. This attire was more commonly worn by 'barbarians' – i.e. people who were not Roman citizens.

Many horsemen were recruited from the edges of empire from tribes and peoples renowned for their cavalry expertise including the Thracians, the Numidians and the Gauls. Lucius' thick brushed-back hair, along with his bushy moustache and beard, offer the viewer further visible clues about his non-Roman background. An account by the ancient writer Diodorus, which describes the manner in which the Gauls style their hair, could well be describing the appearance of Lucius here:

For they are always washing their hair in lime-water, and they pull it back from the forehead to the top of the head and back to the nape of the neck, with the result that their appearance is like that of Satyrs and Pans, since the treatment of their hair makes it so heavy and coarse that it differs in no respect from the mane of horses. Some of them shave the beard, but others let it grow a little; and the nobles shave their cheeks, but they let the moustache grow until it covers the mouth.[31]

The surviving fish-scale pattern across the lower sections of his body suggests he may also be wearing a coverlet of scale armour (*lorica squamata*). This type of armour was often shown on artistic representations of different types of

Fig. 1.2 Tombstone of Aurelius Lucius, on display at the Grosvenor Museum in Chester.

soldiers – from legionaries and auxiliaries to horsemen and standard-bearers – and consisted of small metal scales sewn onto a fabric backing.[32] Behind the figure, we can see the Roman crested helmet with cheek plates, and a sheathed sword. This makes clear to all who pass by his tombstone that he was a military man.

Similarly to the other two dining scenes, a small three-legged table is positioned in front of the couch. But in a variation to the theme, here we also have the figure of a slave standing in front of the couch. The break in the stone has damaged this section of the relief: the slave's head, with rounded eyes and brushed-back hair, remains on the upper fragment while the lower legs and feet appear on the lower fragment. The body is missing but it is clear how the fragments fit together to form a small figure. Enslaved people were often depicted as diminutive in stature across Ancient Greek and Roman art, indicative of their lower status, especially when placed alongside their master or mistress.[33] Here, the slave attends on Aurelius Lucius as he enjoys the banquet. But one of the most striking details on this dining scene is perhaps the object that appears beside the slave's feet: a severed head.

The head faces outwards towards the viewer and the features survive in good detail from the wide eyes and rounded face to the brushed-back hair, closely matching the facial features of the enslaved figure. There is a small protrusion from the top of the head, which some reconstructions interpret as a ponytail by which the slave holds the head aloft. Headhunting – that is, keeping the head of an enemy as a trophy – was not a traditional Roman custom but rather one that was closely associated with the Celts.[34] Indeed, Diodorus records details of the practice among the Gallic tribes with a mix of horror and fascination:

When their enemies fall they cut off their heads and fasten them about the necks of their horses; and turning over to their attendants the arms of their opponents, all covered with blood, they carry them off as booty, singing a paean over them and striking up a song of victory, and these first-fruits of battle they fasten by nails upon their houses, just as men do, in certain kinds of hunting, with the heads of wild beasts they have mastered. The heads of their most distinguished enemies they embalm in cedar-oil and carefully preserve in a chest, and these they exhibit to strangers, gravely maintaining that in exchange for this head some one of their ancestors, or their father, or the man himself, refused the offer of a great sum of money. And some men among them, we are told, boast that they have not accepted an equal weight of gold for the head they show, displaying a barbarous sort of greatness of soul; for not to sell that which constitutes a witness and proof of one's valour is a noble thing, but to continue to fight against one of our own race, after he is dead, is to descend to the level of beasts.[35]

Given the other visual clues about Lucius' nationality on the tombstone, the severed head certainly seems to be confirmation that he is not a Roman by birth. As a skilled horseman, he has been recruited into the Roman army from elsewhere. Although he chooses to be memorialised in the manner of a Roman – the somewhat 'stock' scene of the dinner party plus an inscription in Latin – he nevertheless retains his identity much more visibly than Donatus in the previous tombstone. Anyone passing by Lucius' imposing memorial would, even at a glance, be left in no doubt as to his background or indeed his military prowess as he enjoys an eternal banquet.

MISSING IN ACTION

The tombstones discussed so far give us an insight into how soldiers were memorialised when they died during their time in military service in the province of Britannia. But what about soldiers from Britannia who were sent on active duty elsewhere in the empire? The following tombstone provides an insight into how families of the men who passed away far from home might still memorialise their loved ones, even without being able to bury the body. Reconstructed from several fragments, which were discovered at a farm not far from Isca Silurum fort in the mid-nineteenth century, the large gabled monument is primarily taken up by the inscription, which runs over nine lines.[36] When discovered, the letters retained traces of the original red paint used to mark them out.

Inscription
D M
TADIA VALLAVNIVS VIXIT
ANN LXV ET TADVS EXVPERTVS
FILIVS VIXIT ANN XXXVII DEFVN
TVS EXPEDITIONE GERMANICA
TADIA EXVPERATA FILIA
MATRI ET FRATRI PIISSMA
SECVS TVMVLVM
PATRIS POSVIT

Expanded Text
Dis Manibus
Tadia Vallaunius vixit
annos LXV et Tadius Exuperatus
filius vixit annos XXXVII defunc-
tus expeditione Germanica
Tadia Exuperata filia
matri et fratri piissima
secus tumulum
patris posuit

Translation
TO THE SPIRITS OF THE DEAD
Tadia Vallaunius lived 65 years
and her son Tadius Exuperatus
lived 37 years. He died
on the German expedition.
Tadia Exuperata, most dutiful daughter,
placed this monument to her
mother and brother beside
her father's burial mound.

Rather than a memorial for an individual soldier, here we have two members of the same family commemorated on the same monument: a mother, Tadia Vallaunius, and her son, Tadius Exuperatus. The stone has been erected by another member of the same family, Tadia Exuperata, the daughter and sister of the two named deceased. From these details, we can see that the two children have taken the family name from their mother (Tadia) with their other name presumably then having come from their father (Exuperatus).[37] This family would have likely lived in the civilian settlement (*canabae legionis*) that developed beside the legionary fortress at Isca Silurum. The mention of the father's burial place also being in the same location suggests he may well have been a legionary soldier himself, who married a local woman (Vallaunius is a female Celtic name) and started a family. As we saw above with the tombstone of Julius Julianus, the Second Legion Augusta was based at this fortress for the majority of its time in Britannia.

The tombstone has presumably been erected on the passing of 65-year-old Tadia Vallaunius and would have originally marked the burial place of her remains. But her passing has offered the opportunity to memorialise the deceased son and brother Tadius Exuperatus at the same time. Here we gain a small insight into his military life: we know that he served as a soldier as the inscription tells us that he died (*defunctus*) while away on a military expedition in some part of Germania. Detachments from the Second Legion Augusta were often sent across the province to support campaigns, quell rebellions and assist with building projects, so it is certainly possible that certain detachments may also have been sent further afield when reinforcements were needed during times of unrest.

Without any clear information on his unit or the date of his death, it is difficult to pin down a specific expedition during which Tadius Exuperatus met his demise. Some have suggested the campaigns of the emperor Caracalla on the German frontiers in AD 213–214, for which he earned the title *Germanicus*.[38] Although it is not possible to definitively identify his expedition, it is nonetheless notable that we have his death – while away on military service in another part of the empire – recorded for posterity on a tombstone back in his family's location. If he had died during a battle in some part of Germania, his body would have been collected along with all the other fallen soldiers and either buried or cremated near to the battlefield site without any permanent or indeed individual grave marker.[39] How were his family notified of his death abroad? The Roman army was highly bureaucratic: records of unit numbers and deployment were kept, as were the numbers of dead and their names.[40] Official dispatches would have been sent back to his unit at the fortress, and the family would have been notified by letter or, perhaps in this case given their proximity to the fort, by word of mouth from his comrades.[41]

VETERANS

After serving in the army for at least twenty-five years, soldiers could receive their discharge papers. This was an especially significant occasion for auxiliaries as this was the point at which they would be awarded full Roman citizenship. As tombstones show, many auxiliary and legionary veterans stayed in Britannia after completing their service rather than return home to their native lands. Some settled here with families or had simply become used to life in the province – many men would not have seen their own homeland in decades.

Early in the nineteenth century, eight Roman tombstones were discovered at the orchard at Great Bulmore, where they had been reused as paving. This site lies just over 1 mile from the legionary fortress of Isca Silurum, home to the Second Legion Augusta from the late first century AD onwards. The eight stones seem to have originally belonged to a communal tomb at the site, which contained evidence of urns, cremated remains, burnt bones and a single coin.[42] Two of the eight tombstones recorded the passing of veterans from the Second Legion Augusta who had evidently not strayed far from the fortress after their retirement.

The first of these two veterans is a man identified as Gaius Julius Decuminus.[43] His tombstone is damaged, particularly along the top where it has been broken across the initial two letters D M. Fortunately, the rest of the inscription survives in full.

Inscription	**Expanded Text**
D M	*Dis Manibus*
C IVLI	*Gai Juli*
DECVM	*Decum-*
INII V L II A	*ini[i] veterani legionis II Augusta*
A XXXXV	*annorum XXXXV*
C F C	*coniunx faciendum curavit*

Translation
TO THE SPIRITS OF THE DEAD
For Gaius Julius
Decuminus
veteran of the Second Legion Augusta
45 years old
his wife took care to set this up

The monument is simple in its design and execution. The majority of the inscription is placed within a carved ansate panel: the lettering is haphazard, though some attempt has been made to centre and space it accordingly. The stonecutter has used interpuncts to mark the spaces between different words;

the first of these is almost wishbone-shaped, though they become narrower as the epitaph proceeds. The deceased is identified by his *tria nomina* – Gaius Julius Decuminus. We are not given his filiation or his voting tribe, even though he is clearly a Roman citizen. Instead, he is next identified as a *veteranus* ('veteran') of the Second Legion Augusta (here abbreviated fully as L II A). This legion was stationed at Isca Silurum from AD 74/75 until the end of the third century, though, as with many units, was often sent elsewhere in the province during this time. Indeed, the Second Legion Augusta helped with the construction of both Hadrian's Wall (AD 122–125) and the Antonine Wall (AD 138–142). The inscription records Decuminus' age at the time of death as 45, which, given the minimum of twenty-five years' service, means he was not long retired when he passed away. His tombstone has been erected by his wife, though her name is not recorded.

The second legionary veteran commemorated in this communal tomb was a man called Julius Valens. His inscription is neatly spaced and centred on the stone, with a confident flourish to the letters and small decorative elements added to either side. The stonecutter has also added small triangular interpuncts to separate every word, including at the end and beginning of each separate line, leaving some of the words and abbreviated letters with a double interpunct.

Inscription	Expanded Text
[D M]	*[Dis Manibus]*
IVL VALENS VET	*Julius Valens veteranus*
LEG II AVG VIXIT	*legionis II Augustae vixit*
ANNIS C IVL	*annis C Iulia*
SECVNDINA CONIUNX	*Secundina coniunx*
ET IVL MARTINVS FILIVS	*et Julius Martinus filius*
F C	*faciendum curavit*

Translation

TO THE SPIRITS OF THE DEAD
Julius Valens veteran
of the Second Legion Augusta
he lived 100 years
Julia Secundina his wife
and Julius Martinus his son
took care to set this up

The stone had been broken across the top at some point, which has likely led to the loss of the initial abbreviation D M. Six of the seven other tombstones from the same location all preserve this invocation to the spirits of the dead at the beginning of their epitaphs, while the seventh has similarly lost the top section of stone.[44] We are given slightly more information about the deceased this time: he is identified as Julius Valens, also a *veteranus* ('veteran') of the Second Legion Augusta. However, this time the age recorded tells us that Valens had certainly stayed near Isca Silurum for a long time after his retirement: he had lived until the impressive – and perfectly rounded – sum of 100 years old. Whether this is accurate or not is impossible to tell, but he must have been of advanced enough age for it to seem like a reasonable estimate.

Valens' memorial has been erected by his surviving family: a wife named Julia Secundina and a son named Julius Martinus. The family had evidently remained in the civilian settlement outside the legionary fort after the husband's retirement – perhaps the son, at this point, was completing his own service to the same legion. Interestingly, the tombstone for Julia Secundina herself was recovered at the exact same site, having been erected in her memory by her son – who, on her tombstone, is named in full as Gaius Julius Martinus.[45] As Allason-Jones notes, a veteran may have made for an especially appealing marriage prospect to any young woman: legionary soldiers in particular had earned a good salary over a fairly long career as well as a lump sum on retirement, and their children would receive full Roman citizenship.[46]

It is not only the legionary veterans who remained in the province until their death. Many of those who served in the auxiliary forces also settled in Britannia after their retirement. Their status as veterans was similarly commemorated on their tombstones. Perhaps fittingly, we shall end this chapter where we began, with a Rotherham red tombstone from Templeborough.[47]

Inscription

DIS MANIBVS CROTO VINDICIS EM
ERITO COH IIII GALLORVM ANNORVM
XXXX MONIMENTVM FECIT FLAVIA PE
REGRINA CONIVNX PIENTISSIMA
MARITO PIENTIS-
SIMO TITVLVM POSVIT

Expanded Text

*Dis Manibus Croto Vindicis emerito
cohortis IIII Gallorum annorum
XXXX monimentum fecit Flavia
Peregrina coniunx pientissima marito
pientissimo titulum posuit*

Translation

TO THE SPIRITS OF THE DEAD
For Crotus, son of Vindex, veteran
of the Fourth Cohort of Gauls
40 years old. Flavia Peregrina, his
most devoted wife, made this monument and
placed this epitaph for her most devoted husband

The lettering is rough and rather densely packed into each line. The initial dedication to the spirits of the dead is not abbreviated here but written in full, suggesting a date in the early second century AD. The deceased is identified by a single name, Crotus, along with his filiation as son of Vindex. Both names evidence his Celtic background: although the name Vindex ('avenger') is Latin, it proved popular with Celts in the Roman world as it could conceal a Celtic name element.[48] Crotus is identified as an *emeritus* rather than a *veteranus*: this term was equivalent in that it indicated a soldier who had retired or been honourably discharged from service. He had been attached to the Fourth Cohort of Gauls, which was based at Templeborough fort early after its transfer to the province. It is interesting that despite his retirement – and thus acquisition of Roman citizenship – he is still identified through the single Celtic name only. Was this a deliberate choice to preserve his original identity or a simple oversight? By contrast, his wife Flavia Peregrina, who is named later in the inscription, bears the expected two names of a woman with Roman citizenship.

Crotus is younger than both of our veterans so far: his age at time of death is recorded as 40. This could be an underestimate of his actual age, rounded down to the nearest whole number. Alternatively, if this is a roughly accurate estimate, then he must have either enlisted at the incredibly young age of

Fig. 1.3 Tombstone of Crotus, son of Vindex, on display at Rotherham Museum.

15 or been discharged early on account of injury or illness. It is recorded that the monument and its accompanying inscription was erected by his wife, named on the epitaph as Flavia Peregrina. Their marital harmony is emphasised through their matching descriptions as *pientissima* and *pientissimo* ('most devoted').

The inscription sits beneath a large full-length portrait of the deceased. The top of the monument has been lost – broken, perhaps, when the slab was later reused as a drain cover in the fort – leaving only the lower portion of the figure.

The figure representing Crotus stands within an arched recess, though only a few details can still be picked out from the surviving stone fragment. His monument must have originally been an impressive sight – and one that contrasts with the roughness of the inscription underneath. He is dressed in a tunic and long cloak, which drapes down beneath his knees in a long triangular fold. The scroll that he holds in his left hand is just about still visible: this represents his will, which he was now allowed to legally possess, having gained his citizenship after his – likely very recent – retirement.

Chapter 2

Military Roles

In addition to the many ordinary soldiers whose lives are commemorated across the province, there is a wide variety of tombstones that offer us an insight into the different roles and career paths available to men within the Roman army. This vast professional military force continually grew and developed over the years, both in structure and administration, as the empire's focus shifted from expansion to defence.[1]

The ordinary legionary soldier (*miles*) had a number of opportunities for promotion within the ranks and appointment to special duties as a *principalis*, which would exempt them from usual camp duties and increase their pay. There were a number of roles covered by this term, both within the century and at the legionary headquarters. For the former, we find a wide variety of roles to which a soldier could be appointed from the *tesserarius* ('password keeper') to the *signifer* ('standard-bearer') and the *optio* ('officer'), while at the legionary headquarters a soldier could find himself working as a *speculator* (a type of special emissary or scout) or *beneficiarius* ('administrator').[2] There were also particularly appealing roles within the imperial army such as the cavalry, who, as well as earning more than the ordinary soldier, were often celebrated with impressive monumental tombstones after their demise.

THE OPTIO

A tombstone from Deva Victrix (Chester) records the passing of an aspiring centurion who was lost at sea.[3] The tombstone itself is now broken, having later been recycled in the construction of Chester's north wall. A partial inscription survives on the bottom half of the stone along with some decorative carvings of structures and foliage.

Inscription

[...]
OPTONIS AD SPEM
ORDINIS > LVCILI
INGENVI QVI
NAVFRAGIO PERIT
S E

Expanded Text

...
optionis ad spem
ordinis > Lucili
Ingenui qui
naufragio perit
situs est

Translation

...
[for] an *optio* in line for promotion
from the century of Lucilius Ingenuus
who perished in a shipwreck
he lies

We no longer have the name of the deceased, though we do find out a little more information about his career. He was an *optio*, a military position that put him second in command to the centurion. We're told that at the time of his death he belonged to the century of a man called Lucilius Ingenuus. If you look closely at the inscription, you can see that the word for century is here indicated by the centurial symbol (>) rather than a letter. There is no surviving information about which unit these men belonged to or where they were sailing. If travelling to or from the fortress at Deva, the most likely option could be the Twentieth Legion, which was stationed there for at least two centuries from AD 88 onwards. However, given the circumstances of his death at sea, some have suggested a link with Agricola's campaigns or even the more naval Second Legion Adiutrix, which was at Deva for just over ten years before the Twentieth Legion arrived there. But of course, given the frustrating lack of detail, it may well be the case that he belonged to another unit travelling to or from another site entirely. There are no other records of Lucilius Ingenuus to help track his unit down.

We are also told our *optio* was *ad spem ordinis*, a useful little note for this tombstone, which tells us that at the time of death the deceased was awaiting promotion in military rank. Why add these career details if his promotion had not yet come to pass? Not only does it let us – as the viewer – know that this man was an experienced soldier, but it also tells us he had performed his duties well and was worthy of respect commensurate with his deserved rank at the time of his death. It also underscores the sudden and unexpected nature of his passing: he perished before he could enjoy the next – and imminent – stage of his military career.

Shipwrecks were a hazard for any seafaring Roman, and the danger only increased as their wooden ships tackled unfamiliar seas. The tombstone does not state whether the shipwreck occurred off the coast of Cheshire on a journey intended to reach Deva or whether it was somewhere

Fig 2.1 Tombstone fragment of an unknown *optio*, on display at the Grosvenor Museum in Chester.

further afield. To date, no Roman shipwrecks have been identified along Britannia's western coast, though modern records from the seventeenth century onwards certainly attest to the dangers around the area – particularly vessels foundered or lost in the Dee Estuary, a route that Roman ships would likely use to reach Deva.

There is a slight alteration to one of the customary sentiments at the end of the *optio*'s epitaph. Instead of the abbreviation HSE, here we find only the second and third letters, S and E. The full abbreviation stands for *hic situs est* – 'here he lies' – but with the body presumably lost to the waves and not buried beneath the tombstone, the 'here' – *hic* – has been left off the inscription this time. Perhaps, given the spacing, it was expected to be added in later when the body was recovered. Or perhaps it was meant to simply acknowledge the further loss that arises from disasters at sea: the body lies *somewhere*, but it is not *here*. That our unnamed *optio* was commemorated with this tombstone despite the lack of a body to bury is another testament to the honour afforded to him, whether by his comrades or by his family.

A simple scene is carved underneath the inscription. In the middle is a large structure with pointed gable roof and closed double doors. The gable is decorated with a small crescent moon. On either side of the central building are two smaller structures in the same general style, though without doors and without the crescent moon decoration. Leafy plants grow in front of both smaller buildings. This could be a depiction of a simple but idyllic Roman tomb – perhaps the kind of grand funerary structure our *optio* may have received had he lived a longer life and passed away closer to home.

THE CORNICULARIUS

Records from the eighteenth century describe a tombstone for a *cornicularius*, which was discovered at Aesica (Great Chesters) fort.[4] Aesica was a small fort built on the site of one of the earlier milecastles (Milecastle 43). To the south-east of the fort itself was a civilian settlement (*vicus*), and to the south of this lay a cemetery. Seven tombstones have been recovered from the site so far – although not all have survived to the modern day. This particular tombstone was lost early in the nineteenth century, but its details were discussed and even sketched in several antiquarian accounts. The inscription is set within a simple panel and records basic information about the deceased, which, although brief, offers a small glimpse into some of the different military roles within the administrative sphere.

Inscription	**Expanded Text**
D M	*Dis Manibus*
AEL MERCV	*Aelio Mercuriali*
RIALI CORNICVL	*corniculario*
VACIA SOROR FECIT	*Vacia soror fecit*

Translation
TO THE SPIRITS OF THE DEAD
For Aelius Mercurialis
cornicularius
his sister Vacia made this

After the customary dedication to the spirits of the dead, we have the name of the deceased given as Aelius Mercurialis. Here it is given in the dative case (visible in the unabbreviated *Mercuriali* across the second to third lines) to indicate the monument is also dedicated to him.

Next, we are told that Mercurialis was a *cornicularius*. This was a senior administrative role within the military unit, named after a small horn (*corniculum*) worn on their helmet.[5] As a term, it is often conveyed in English as 'senior clerk'. The *cornicularius* oversaw many administrative duties within the military unit from the general organisation of the clerical staff to the management of supplies and the verification of paperwork.[6] In the military context, he was a senior soldier just below the rank of centurion; evidence shows that men who occupied this role could then be promoted to the office of *optio ad spem ordinis* as well as centurion.[7] Each unit would have one *cornicularius* on the staff to manage its fairly complex administration.

The final line of the inscription provides details on the monument's dedicator. In this case, the tombstone has been set up by a woman called Vacia who is identified as Mercurialis' sister (*soror*). Given that Mercurialis' sister was present at the site to organise his burial, it has been suggested that Mercurialis had possibly been recruited into the unit from a local Romano-British family.[8] In the early second century AD, Aesica was briefly home to the Sixth Cohort of Nervii. This was an infantry unit originally raised from among the Nervii in Gallia Belgica (modern-day Belgium). By the third century, Aesica was garrisoned by the First Cohort of Asturians. This was a mixed infantry and cavalry auxiliary unit from the Astures peoples in northern Hispania (modern-day Spain).

THE CENTURION

One of the best-known roles within the Roman army is the legionary centurion, often considered the backbone of the legion.[9] As the principal professional officer in the army, the centurion occupied an important link between the higher command and the common soldiers.[10] The centurion commanded a unit called a century (*centuria*) which, during the time of the empire, consisted of eighty soldiers. Six centuries made a cohort and ten cohorts made a legion, therefore each legion had a total of sixty centurions.

A legionary centurion could progress through the ranks until reaching the most senior role within the legion of *prior primus pilus*. This post earned at least fifteen times the pay of a common soldier, making it a particularly attractive goal for many men. A large proportion of centurions were recruited from among the legionary troops based on their military expertise and achievements: these men would have had to serve in junior officer roles – just like the *optio* on the previous tombstone – before being promoted to the centurion level of command. However, during the imperial period an increasing number of men also transferred into the post from the municipal magistracy and the equestrian ranks, attracted by the high pay and potential for furthering their careers. Centurions are also found in the auxiliary units, though these 'less prestigious' officers are often overlooked.[11] Auxiliary centurions were recruited from among their own cohorts, which offered a unique – if small – path of progression for a non-Roman citizen. For while the legionary centurion could progress further beyond this post, auxiliary centurions mostly remained at this level for the duration of their military careers.

The centurion was responsible for the training, management and administration of the men within his century. This included discipline, for which the centurion had his very own tool: a staff made of vinewood (*vitis*). The centurion carried this with him, using it during military exercises as well as for meting out punishment.[12] The Roman writer Pliny the Elder described how the *vitis* became a symbol of supreme authority and command – and as we shall see in some of the examples below, it also appears in depictions of the centurion on funerary monuments as a key visual marker of their role.[13]

VIVIUS MARCIANUS
SECOND LEGION AUGUSTA

From among the ruins of St Martin Ludgate church, destroyed in the Great Fire of London in 1666, emerged the unmistakeable form of a Roman soldier who had been carved in stone centuries beforehand in ancient Londinium. Several accounts describe the monument as having been discovered by Sir Christopher Wren during his renovation work at the site in 1669; it was then moved to Oxford for display with assistance from the Archbishop of Canterbury.[14] While the 2-metre-high limestone monument had miraculously survived in one full piece, the surface was badly worn. Several dowel holes and a cramp socket on the stone's front indicate that it had later been recycled as building material so was doubtless recovered away from its original location.

The tombstone features a full-length 1.2-metre-tall portrait of a soldier set within an arched recess. Unlike many of the examples we have seen so far, the accompanying inscription is set above the relief rather than beneath it. Despite some extensive incisions across the surface, the epitaph is still legible.

<table>
<tr><td align="center">Inscription</td><td align="center">Expanded Text</td></tr>
<tr><td align="center">D M</td><td align="center">Dis Manibus</td></tr>
<tr><td align="center">VIVIO MARCI</td><td align="center">Vivio Marciano</td></tr>
<tr><td align="center">ANO > LEG II</td><td align="center">centurio legionis II</td></tr>
<tr><td align="center">AVG IANVARIA</td><td align="center">Augusta Ianuaria</td></tr>
<tr><td align="center">MARTINA CONIVNX</td><td align="center">Martina coniunx</td></tr>
<tr><td align="center">PIENTISSIMA POSV</td><td align="center">pientissima posuit</td></tr>
<tr><td align="center">IT MEMORIAM</td><td align="center">memoriam</td></tr>
</table>

Translation
TO THE SPIRITS OF THE DEAD
For Vivius Marcianus
centurion of the Second Legion
Augusta. Januaria
Martina, his most devoted wife,
set this up in his memory

The letters are a little haphazard in style, contrasting with the large elaborate relief below. Triangular interpuncts separate the words on each line; there is also a small ivy leaf interpunct carved after the ending of the name Marcianus. His status as a centurion is indicated by the appearance of the remnants of a centurial sign (>) just before – or colliding with – this interpunct. Two ligatures appear (TI, RI) in the name Martina and the final word *memoriam*. There are also a couple of occasions where the stonemason has inserted a smaller letter inside the letter C either as a stylistic quirk or to correct minor spelling errors: thus, there is a small I inserted inside the C of *Marciano* and a small O inside the C of *coniunx*.

The inscription provides the customary abbreviated address to the spirits of the dead, followed by some details on the deceased. We learn that our soldier is called Vivius Marcianus and is a centurion from the Second Legion Augusta. Vivius is an alternative spelling of the more common Vibius. We are not told how long he had served in the military for, nor his age at the time of death, but we do know that his impressive monument was erected by his dearly devoted (*pientissima*) wife, Januaria Martina. As a centurion, Marcianus would have been able to legally marry.

What brought Vivius Marcianus to Londinium? As we noted when looking at the tombstone of Julius Julianus, a soldier from the same legion, the Second Legion Augusta spent the majority of its time in Britannia stationed at Isca Silurum (Caerleon) in modern-day South Wales. Detachments could be sent across the province to assist with many other matters from uprisings and building works to secondments for the provincial governor.[15] Londinium had originally been established as a small settlement following the Claudian invasion in AD 43, but was completely destroyed during the Boudiccan revolt of AD 60/61. In no short time, however, it was rebuilt and strengthened, and by the end of the first century AD had undergone a period of rapid expansion, which led to it becoming the province's largest city: as a result, it soon replaced Camulodunum (Colchester) as the provincial capital. By the late second century, growth had slowed and the population began to decrease again. Marcianus may have been sent to Londinium – either by himself or as part of a detachment – to undertake work for the provincial governor. A fragmentary monument to another soldier from the Second Legion Augusta, Lucius Valerius Celsus, was discovered in Blackfriars in 1843.[16] Celsus' monument also features the relief of a figure, though the lower sections below the head are now lost, positioned beneath an inscription. Interestingly, on the epitaph, Celsus is identified as a *speculator* from the Second Legion Augusta; the three men who were responsible for erecting the monument are also named on the epitaph and identified as *speculatores*. The term *speculator* describes a legionary who was seconded to the governor to serve as a special emissary. Over time, this role evolved from scouting and reconnaissance missions to include bodyguard duties and military policing activities;[17] this must be what has brought Celsus from Isca Silurum to Londinium in the early half of the second century AD.[18]

Returning to Marcianus' tombstone, his full-length 1.2-metre funerary portrait may be worn but many of its elaborate details can still be appreciated. The figure stands within the recess, facing the viewer directly, leaning slightly on the vine staff (*vitis*) in his right hand. He is dressed in a short belted tunic, which is partially covered by a long cloak. The cloak is fastened at the right shoulder and sweeps across his chest, falling in meticulously carved folds over and behind his left arm all the way down to his calves. The details on the face do not survive. His left hand holds a scroll while his right hand, as mentioned, holds the *vitis*, the vine staff of the centurion. Writing tablets or implements often appear on military tombstones to indicate the deceased's expertise in administrative matters; the scroll alone – as here – is thought to represent the deceased's will. The hefty *vitis* upon which he leans visibly confirms his military rank to passers-by, emphasising his status and importance even in death.

MARCUS FAVONIUS FACILIS
TWENTIETH LEGION

Over at Camulodunum, another centurion has withstood the passage of time. Marcus Favonius Facilis' tombstone was discovered on the west side of the city in 1868.[19] Broken in two, it lay 1 metre beneath the surface. A lead urn, still containing cremated human remains, was discovered nearby along with some small grave goods.

The tombstone had once stood in the cemetery that bordered the main road to Londinium from the south-west of the fortress-turned-*colonia*, but it had not lasted long before it was suddenly broken and buried. As it had spent such little time exposed to the elements, the tombstone had survived in remarkably good condition. Measuring almost 2 metres tall, the upper portion features a large full-length portrait of Facilis standing within an arched recess in his military attire. Directly underneath the figure is the epitaph, which has survived in full. It is thought to be one of the earliest Roman sculptures to survive from the province.[20]

Inscription	Expanded Text
M FAVONI M F POL FACI	*Marcus Favonius Marci filius Pollia*
LIS > LEG XX VERECVND	*Facilis centurio legionis XX Verecundus*
VS ET NOVICIVS LIB POSV	*et Novicius liberti posuerunt*
ERVNT H S E	*hic situs est*

Translation
Marcus Favonius Facilis, son of Marcus, from the Pollian voting tribe
centurion in the Twentieth Legion
Verecundus and Novicius, his freedmen, set this up
HERE HE LIES

There is no dedication to the spirits of the dead at the start of the inscription, which suggests an earlier date in the first century AD. The first line identifies the deceased by his *tria nomina* along with his filiation (M F) and his voting tribe (POL). As a Roman citizen, Marcus Favonius Facilis belongs to the Pollian voting tribe, which enables him to cast a vote in elections. The next line provides some information on his military career: the appearance of the centurial symbol (>) once again makes clear that he was a centurion within the Twentieth Legion (LEG XX). Notably, the legion is not given its honorific title *Valeria Victrix* (VV) here. This also points to an earlier date for the tombstone having been set up in the earliest years of the Roman occupation in the first century AD, as it is commonly believed that the title was bestowed in recognition of the legion's success in quelling the Boudiccan revolt in AD 60/61.

The monument has been erected by two of the deceased's freedmen (LIB = *liberti*) rather than his comrades or family members. Both are named here as Verecundus and Novicius. Freedmen and freedwomen were former slaves who had been legally freed through a process known as manumission. Freed slaves were no longer property but citizens with their own rights, though there were restrictions placed upon their status – for example, they could not hold office. Freedmen and freedwomen also remained bound to their former master (now known as their patron) in many ways: they were required to follow a set of rules around deference and obedience (*obsequium*) as well as offer services (*operae*) – which, as here, could include the care of their funerary arrangements after death.[21] Any children born to freedmen and freedwomen after their manumission were considered freeborn citizens and were not subject to any legal restrictions. In Chapters 3 and 4, we will see more examples of freedmen and freedwomen through the tombstones they themselves left behind.

Roman slaves usually had only one name, signifying their status as property rather than individuals. On being freed, both men would have customarily taken the praenomen and nomen of their former master as well as an alternate form of filiation that identified their status as *liberti*. They would keep their former slave name as their cognomen. Formally written, then, the full names of the two freedmen mentioned here would be Marcus Favonius M(arci) L(ibertus) Verecundus and Marcus Favonius M(arcus) L(ibertus) Novicius.

Neither full name is recorded in this case, perhaps to save space and cost, or perhaps because it was simply not deemed important enough to be recorded as it could be easily inferred.

The impressive full-length portrait of Facilis takes up more than half of the stone's surface. The composition of the scene matches that of our previous centurion Marcianus: Facilis stands within an arched recess, facing the viewer directly, and holds the centurion's vine staff in his right hand. This tombstone, however, has survived in significantly better condition and preserves the work of a much more skilled artist: the eternally youthful Facilis is shown in the idealised Julio-Claudian style in his full military attire. He wears a cuirass over a uniformly pleated tunic, all girded by a highly decorated belt. He holds the pommel of his sword (*gladius*), which hangs from a baldric, and wears his dagger (*pugio*) on his right hip. A long cloak is draped from his left shoulder and wraps elegantly around his left arm, falling over his left hand and down past his knees. His outfit is completed with greaves and boots. The detail and quality of the portrait is remarkable and bears many similarities to military tombstones from the Rhineland. Recent petrological analysis has also revealed that the stone used for this tombstone had been imported: the material was identified as Lothringer freestone from the eastern area of Gaul, where military quarrying is known to have taken place.[22] Before their arrival in Britain, the Twentieth Legion had been stationed at Novaesium in Germania Inferior. Here, they had been using the same stone – the Lothringer freestone – for their monuments, which has led many to conclude that Facilis' tombstone was created by a continental stonemason there before the legion was moved.[23]

As we noted previously with the tombstone of Furius Maximus, the Twentieth Legion had accompanied the emperor Claudius on his initial invasion of Britannia in AD 43. During the years after the invasion, it was based at Camulodunum, where it constructed the province's first legionary fortress. The legion remained there until AD 49. Following its departure, Camulodunum was developed into the province's first *colonia*, a town in which army veterans settled with their families on their newly granted land. Given that Facilis is not identified as a veteran on the tombstone, it seems more likely that he was still serving as a centurion at the time of his death. This helpfully then narrows down the period during which Facilis' tombstone would have been erected to a much shorter span of six years between invasion and the legion's departure from Camulodunum. But this still leaves the question of why Facilis' tombstone ended up broken and buried not long after it was erected in the cemetery. What happened?

The Boudiccan revolt mentioned above may have had something to do with it. Camulodunum at this time was the provincial capital, making it a prime target for the uprising led by the Iceni and their allies against their Roman occupiers. The Iceni were an ancient Iron Age tribe whose territory covered part of the eastern side of Britain – roughly modern-day Norfolk and part of Suffolk. The Iceni had agreed to an alliance with the Roman forces following their invasion, though relations had been fraught: an unpopular policy of disarmament introduced by the provincial governor Publius Ostorius Scapula led to the first unsuccessful Iceni revolt in AD 47. Ostorius followed this up in AD 49 by seizing more land for the new *colonia* at Camulodunum, a site that only served to heighten the tension between the Romans and the native peoples. The historian Tacitus describes how the ongoing colonisation only encouraged further violence:

> The bitterest animosity was felt against the veterans; who, fresh from their settlement in the colony of Camulodunum, were acting as though they had received a free gift of the entire country, driving the natives from their homes, ejecting them from their lands,—they styled them 'captives' and 'slaves',—and abetted in their fury by the troops, with their similar mode of life and their hopes of equal indulgence. More than this, the temple raised to the deified Claudius continually met the view, like the citadel of an eternal tyranny.[24]

When the pro-Roman king of the Iceni, Prasutagus, died in AD 60, he left behind a will that stipulated that half of his kingdom was to be inherited by his two daughters rather than fully to the emperor, as was the expectation for client kingdoms. This was not upheld by Decianus Catus, the procurator at the time. Instead, the entirety of the Iceni royal family's estate – land, money, treasures, even livestock – was sequestered by the Romans. Heavy taxes were imposed on the Iceni people and much of their land was seized. Boudicca was beaten, her two daughters were raped, and many of Prasutagus' family were enslaved. In response to this cavalcade of outrages against her family and people, Boudicca raised a large army from the Iceni and neighbouring tribes, which allegedly numbered into the hundreds of thousands.[25] Their first target was the nearest bastion of Roman imperial rule: Camulodunum.

As a *colonia* now instead of a legionary fortress, Camulodunum was unprepared for the attack. The now unwalled settlement – even with the 2,000 or so veterans who lived there – was not prepared to withstand an attack. The citizens sent an urgent appeal to the procurator Decianus Catus for help: in response, he sent a detachment of 200 light infantry soldiers. A contingent from the Ninth Legion was also dispatched from Longthorpe under the command of the legate Petillius Cerialis. This unit of 2,000 or so legionaries was ambushed on its way and almost entirely wiped out: all were slaughtered save a single infantry soldier along with Cerialis and the cavalry section.[26] Camulodunum held out for two days against the attack before it was defeated. Boudicca's army massacred the inhabitants and razed the entire settlement to the ground.[27] This is the point at which our tombstone re-enters the narrative after a bit of a diversion: Marcus Favonius Facilis, a stark symbol of Roman rule and subjugation, standing in his eternal duty along the road outside the town, would have certainly been toppled and trampled into the ground during the onslaught of Boudicca's army. It is fitting for Facilis, then, that his comrades in the Twentieth Legion played such an integral role in Boudicca's eventual defeat.

AMMONIUS
FIRST COHORT OF HISPANIA

During seventeenth-century investigations of the Roman fort at Ardoch in modern-day Scotland, a tombstone was recovered. The buff sandstone monument measures just over 0.5 metres wide by 0.7 metres tall, and had been reused in later building on the site.[28] It features an inscription set within a simple panel. There is no additional decoration or relief, making it rather less extravagant than the previous two centurions' monuments.

Inscription
DIS MANIBVS
AMMONIVSDA
MIONIS > COH
IHISPANORVM
STIPENDIORVM
XXVIIHEREDES
F C

Expanded Text
Dis Manibus
Ammonius Damionis
centurio cohortis
I Hispanorum
stipendiorum
XXVII heredes
faciendum curaverunt

Translation
TO THE SPIRITS OF THE DEAD
Ammonius son of Damio
centurion of the First Cohort of
Hispania
27 years' service
his heirs took care to set this up

The first line contains the standard invocation to the spirits of the dead. It is not abbreviated here but written in its full form – *Dis Manibus* – a habit that was most popular in the first century AD. Following this, we get a standard list of information about the deceased. He is identified by one single name written in full in the nominative form – Ammonius. The single name indicates he was not yet a Roman citizen despite his lengthy military service, while the name itself suggests his family origins lay to the east of the empire.[29] Ammon was the Hellenised and Romanised spelling of Amun, a major Egyptian god. Amun was adopted into Greek then Roman worship through syncretism as Zeus Ammon/Jupiter Ammon.

Next, we are given the deceased's filiation as 'son of Damio'. We do not have the expected F (= *filio*) abbreviation alongside the second name to clearly signal this, but the second name is given in the genitive form (*Damionis*). This carries the meaning 'of or belonging to Damio', differentiating it from the first name Ammonius. It may seem awkward when written in full like this, but it is a typical alternative for identifying an individual's father.

Over the next few lines, we find out a bit more about Ammonius' military career. The centurial symbol (>) appears after the word DAMIONIS to indicate his military rank as centurion. We are also told the unit to which he belonged: Cohors I Hispanorum (COH I HISPANORUM). This stands for the First Cohort of Hispania, a part-mounted auxiliary unit drawn from modern-day Spain. Inscriptions place it in Britannia shortly after the emperor Hadrian's visit in AD 122, and it was stationed in the north of the province with a particularly strong presence at Alauna (Maryport) and later Castra Exploratorum (Netherby). This tombstone is the first evidence to place anyone from the unit this far north in the province.

Ardoch fort had three key periods of occupation: first, when it was established during Agricola's campaigns towards the end of the first century AD, as part of a series of forts and camps that stretched across the Gask Ridge between modern-day Dunblane and Perth.[30] The fort was reoccupied around AD 140–158 and again in AD 158–163, when attempts were made to push beyond the established frontier. Given the style of the tombstone is very much of the first century AD, Ammonius must have died at Ardoch during its first occupation.

Ammonius' age at the time of death is not given, though his number of years' service is recorded as twenty-seven. Auxiliary soldiers during this period had to serve *at least* twenty-five years before retiring, so it may be the case that Ammonius was subject to a longer term of service, especially given his role as centurion, or was not yet ready to retire – perhaps he aspired to a higher-ranking position. His memorial has been erected by his heirs (plural), though their names are not recorded; given the remoteness of the military location in this case, it seems likely his heirs were fellow soldiers. It may not carry the same gravitas as the tombstones of the two legionary soldiers we previously considered, but nevertheless, this simple monument, standing for several decades outside the abandoned fort in the remote frontier wilderness, would have made for a sombre scene indeed.

THE MEDIC

Back along Hadrian's Wall, near windswept Vercovicium (Housesteads) fort, stood a memorial for a young doctor by the name of Anicius Ingenuus.[31] One of sixteen forts built on Hadrian's Wall, Vercovicium was home to around 800 men. A fairly extensive civilian settlement (*vicus*) also developed outside the fort's walls. Vercovicium originally followed a typical rectangular fort layout, featuring an assortment of central buildings flanked by the barrack blocks. The central buildings included the headquarters (*principia*), the commanding officer's residence (*praetorium*) and granaries. At this fort – like a handful of others along the wall – archaeologists also discovered the remains of a large building with a courtyard, next to the *principia*. This has been identified as the fort's hospital (*valetudinarium*) – a place Anicius Ingenuus would have known well.

The tombstone stands just over 1.5 metres tall, and has survived in a generally good condition. To the top of the monument is a small decorative relief featuring a hare. Underneath, in a recessed panel, is the inscription. The panel occupies more than half of the stone, with the inscription running across seven well-spaced uniform lines. When discovered, the tombstone had been broken into two large pieces, which caused some damage across the second and third lines of the inscription. Fortunately, this was not too extensive, and the lettering is still entirely legible.

Inscription	Expanded Text
D M	*Dis Manibus*
ANICIO	*Anicio*
INGENVO	*Ingenuo*
MEDICO	*medico*
ORD COH	*ordinario cohortis*
I TVNGR	*I Tungrorum*
VIX AN XXV	*vixit annos XXV*

Translation
TO THE SPIRITS OF THE DEPARTED
For Anicius Ingenuus
serving doctor
of the First Cohort of Tungrians
he lived 25 years

The monument is dedicated to the spirits of the dead as well as the deceased himself, here named as Anicius Ingenuus. We are not given information about his origins; instead, the inscription provides a brief description of his role within his unit and his age at the time of death. No information is provided about who set up the monument.

Anicius is identified as a *medicus ordinarius* for the First Cohort of Tungrians. This was a medical posting within the army: *medicus* is the Latin for doctor, while *ordinarius* is an indicator of his rank. There has been much disagreement over how best to interpret this term: most consider it to refer specifically to a military doctor who held the rank of centurion.[32] Military doctors were considered to be soldiers themselves, and as members of the army, took the military oath.[33] That is not to say they were active combatants but they were assimilated within the army and fort structures. In the legionary forts, the *medicus castrorum* or *castrensis* ('fort doctor') was in charge of medical care and management of all other medical staff in the fort hospital. At an auxiliary fort like Vercovicium, Anicius was likely the most senior medical figure and would have been expected to carry out a number of responsibilities from general practitioner duties to direct interventions like surgery.[34]

The First Cohort of Tungrians garrisoned Vercovicium from the second century AD until the fourth century. They were an auxiliary unit of 800 infantry soldiers, originally recruited from the Tungri people whose territories were incorporated first into the province of Gallia Belgica and later Germania Inferior. While we are not given details on Anicius Ingenuus' home, many of those trained in medicine during the years of the Roman Empire had Greek origins, and indeed some have suggested Anicius Ingenuus could have been the freeborn son of a Greek freedman.[35] Even though he died at the young age of 25, he may have had several years of medical experience. Medical training was not formalised at this point and a large part of any physician's development was based on experience; one can imagine that Anicius Ingenuus' posting at a busy frontier fort would have provided plenty of opportunities for learning on the job. One of the many wooden writing tablets recovered from the nearby fort at Vindolanda preserves a military strength report for the First Cohort of Tungrians for the years AD 92–97 while it was stationed there.[36] The list includes tallies for men who are *aegri* ('sick') and *uolnerati* ('wounded'), as well as those suffering from *lippientes* ('eye inflammation').

Above the inscription sits a neatly carved hare, crouching beneath an arch of leaves. The hare often appears on Romano-British art of many different forms, from jewellery to mosaics, pottery to stone reliefs, blending their prevalence across both the Roman and Celtic worlds. What symbolism does it carry as the main imagery on this tombstone? As with many ancient symbols, without a clear statement on its inherent meaning it is difficult to know for sure. Many Greek and Roman writers linked the hare with Aphrodite or Venus, their goddess of love and fertility, on account of its own fecundity as well as its ability to incite love when offered as a gift.[37] It could be used here to represent love and affection for the deceased. Equally, given the hare's propensity for creating life, it could represent vitality and the cyclicality of life and death. Or perhaps Anicius had earned a hare-inspired nickname owing to his own qualities – in love, in agility, in cunning – or his own hunting interests.

Hares also have relevance to Anicius Ingenuus' role as doctor. The hare appears in the Hippocratic corpus, an expansive collection of Ancient Greek treatises on medicine, as a key ingredient in many ancient medical treatments – for example, a paste made from ground hare's head and mice is recommended as a remedy for gum disease in women.[38]

But there could also be a simpler explanation as the hare was also a popular choice for a pet in Britannia even before the arrival of the Romans. Caesar noted in his own writing that the Britons did not eat hare (or fowl or goose) but preferred to keep them as a 'source of delight'.[39] Perhaps, then, it was simply meant to represent exactly what it looks like: a hare.

THE TRIBUNE

The rural nature of much of the Roman frontier across modern-day Northumberland means that sometimes finds appear during routine farming activity like ploughing. This was the case with the next tombstone, discovered near Bremenium (High Rochester) fort, an outpost that lay 20 miles north of Hadrian's Wall.[40] The 'curious though imperfect' tombstone lay in a wheat field opposite the north-east corner of the fort, where it was observed and recorded in the early nineteenth century.[41] Several stone tombs have been discovered at the site. The surviving sandstone forms a simple gabled monument, almost 1 metre high by 0.8 metres wide, covered with an extensive inscription. The first few lines had been especially badly damaged and weathered away to an irrecoverable degree; indeed, a laminated sign accompanying the stone in its current location at St Cuthbert's Church in Elsdon records how these letters 'came off in flakes' when it was lifted. Despite this, the remaining nine lines still offer a wealth of information about the deceased.

Inscription	Expanded Text
[...] S	*Dis Manibus Sacrum*
[...]	*[...]*
[..] HII [...] I [...] II [...] II	*[...]*
[..] COH I VARDVL [...]	*cohortis I Vardullorum*
[..PRAE..] COH I AVG	*[praefecto] cohortis I Augustae*
LVSITANOR ITEM COH I	*Lusitanorum item cohortis I*
BREVCOR SVBCVR VIAE	*Breucorum subcuratori viae*
FLAMINAE ET ALIMENT	*Flaminiae et alimentorum*
SVBCVR OPERVM PVBL	*subcuratori operum publicorum*
IVLIA LVCILLA C F MARITO	*Iulia Lucilla clarissima femina marito*
B M VIX AN XLVIII	*bene merenti vixit annos XLVIII*
M VI D XXV	*menses VI dies XXV*

Translation

TO THE SACRED SPIRITS OF THE DEAD
[...]
[...]
of the First Cohort of Vardulli
prefect of the First Cohort Augusta
of Lusitanians as well as of the First Cohort
of Breuci, subcurator of the
Flaminian Way and Welfare
subcurator of Public Works
Julia Lucilla, a woman from the senatorial rank,
set this up for her well-deserving husband
he lived 48 years
6 months and 25 days

We can see from the textual damage indicated by the square brackets [...] that the name of the deceased has been lost along with some initial information about his occupation. But we then do have a long occupational history followed by the name of the person who set up the monument – his wife, Julia Lucilla. And in a rare stroke of luck, we actually have another inscription from the same site that happens to mention Lucilla and her husband. This is not from a tombstone but another commonly inscribed stone object left behind by the Romans – an altar.

To Silvanus Pantheus
for the health of
Rufinus the tribune and
his wife Lucilla
Eutychus the freedman
with his family
willingly and deservedly fulfilled his vow

Altars were used in religious ceremonies to offer gifts to the gods. This altar from the north-west of the fort site was dedicated to the god Silvanus Pantheus, specifically for the health of Rufinus the tribune and his wife Lucilla. The pairing of the husband and wife again means that at least part of the missing name and occupation on our tombstone can be restored – Rufinus the tribune – though it looks like the appeal for an intervention on Rufinus' health may not have been answered as speedily as Eutychus had hoped.

Returning to Rufinus' tombstone, it is clear from the lengthy inscription that he has had a varied and impressive career across his forty-eight years. The highest and most recent office would usually be listed first to indicate the deceased's role at the time of death, and given the evidence from the altar, this would have been his appointment as tribune. A military tribune was a senior commander within the army whose role ranked above that of centurion. A tribune was usually appointed from the equestrian order (*equites*). This was a social class from which cavalrymen had originally been recruited in Rome's early years; even before the end of the Republic, however, the demands for cavalry far outstripped the number of men available. More and more were drawn from the commoner class and then – as we have already seen on some of the tombstones so far – from among other more skilled foreign peoples they had subjugated. The equestrian order thus became an officer class instead, and under the emperor Augustus was more formally reorganised. The specific criteria are debated but it is generally agreed that all men admitted to the order had to be Roman citizens of free birth who were in possession of at least 400,000 sesterces.[42] During the years of the empire, the *equites* were a second aristocratic order: many became officers for the army or held senior posts within Rome's extensive civil administration.[43] From the surviving inscriptions – as here – we often see that these men held at least three military posts as part of their career progression – prefect of a cohort, military tribune, and prefect of an *ala*.[44]

Rufinus is linked with three units throughout his own military career: the First Cohort of Vardulli, the First Cohort Augusta of Lusitanians and the First Cohort of Breuci. Given the First Cohort of Vardulli was stationed at Bremenium during the third century, it is reasonable to assume this is the auxiliary unit to which he was attached as tribune at the time of his passing. The Vardulli themselves were originally from Hispania Tarraconensis, the modern-day Basque region in northern Spain. This cohort is recorded on inscriptions at several sites across the north of Britannia, in and around both the Antonine Wall and Hadrian's Wall. Before assuming the command of the First Cohort of Vardulli in the north of Britannia, Rufinus had twice served as prefect. He is linked with both the First Cohort Augusta of Lusitanians and the First Cohort of Breuci: the former based in Egypt, the latter in Mauretania Caesariensis (modern-day Algeria).[45]

Interestingly, we discover that Rufinus has also held quite the selection of civic administrative roles during his career. These are also meticulously recorded on his epitaph for posterity. He held appointments as a subcurator, in which he would have directly supported the work of senatorial curators in Rome. This has included providing support for the Flaminian Way, a key road stretching for over 200 miles from Rome to Ariminum (modern-day Rimini) in the north of Italy. He has also worked on welfare distribution as well as public building works.

Why go to the effort of including such a lengthy *curriculum vitae* on the tombstone, when in reality many of the people passing by the tombstone would not have known what most of these roles were? Self-representation was an important part of it – and this not only applied to the deceased but also to their surviving family. You can see this later in the inscription, too, as his wife

Lucilla takes care to describe herself as *clarissima femina*. This term – literally meaning 'esteemed woman' – indicates she was herself from an aristocratic Roman family of the senatorial class. She has married the equestrian Rufinus – from the social class beneath her own – but yet records her own familial background on his tombstone, even though she would have technically 'lost' her rank when she married him.[46] By emphasising her own social standing in this way on Rufinus' epitaph, she is deliberately moulding her own self-image alongside that of her hard-working husband. Lucilla thus ensures that her social peers in and around Bremenium remember both of them in this way.[47]

Compared to some of the other monuments we have seen, the quality and design of the surviving stone and its inscription rather sharply contrast with the carefully curated illustrious standing of both the deceased and his wife. Perhaps this modest monument was hastily commissioned to mark Rufinus' sudden passing and burial far from home and accompanied a built stone tomb in the cemetery. Lucilla would not have been able to stay at the fort after Rufinus' passing and so there would have been no family left at Bremenium to care for an expensive or elaborate grave: she may well have erected a more fitting monument to her 'well-deserving' (*bene merenti*) husband on her return to Rome.

THE VICTORIOUS RIDER

Ancient stonemasons kept a repertoire of popular scenes that were fitting for an individual's final monument. For the *eques*, a skilled horseman in the army, we find the repeated design of the victorious rider, often referred to as the *Reiter* ('Rider') type. More than 200 examples have survived in total from across the Roman Empire, with over 20 of these coming from Britannia. It seems to have been a particularly popular tombstone scene in and around the Rhineland area with at least forty having been identified in Germania Infcrior alone.[48]

The scene is striking, if straightforward: the rider is shown towering over a defeated enemy who lies under the raised front legs of the horse. There are small variations from tombstone to tombstone – whether the soldier's attire, the enemy's demise, or the weapon of choice – but the overall scene arrangement remains the same. It is an interesting visual message for a soldier to leave behind in an occupied land: would an everyday Briton, on passing the tombstone by the roadside, feel more affinity to the conquering soldier or the defeated enemy?

FLAVINUS
PETRIANA CAVALRY WING

Visitors to Hexham Abbey will find an unlikely ancient inhabitant at the foot of the Night Stair: Flavinus the *eques*. His towering tombstone, measuring over 2.5 metres tall, was rediscovered during renovation works in 1881. It had been used face-up in foundation work under the floor of the south transept porch. Many other Roman stone fragments have been recycled in the abbey's building, including a dedication slab, which is still visible today in the ceiling of the crypt. These stones were likely gathered from the remains of nearby Coria (Corbridge) fort during the construction of the early Anglo-Saxon abbey in the seventh century BC. One benefit of the stone recycling on this occasion is that Flavinus' tombstone has survived in one piece, an unbroken monolith of buff sandstone.

The tombstone features an impressive relief of a victorious rider, which occupies more than half the stone's surface. Underneath it, set within an ansate panel, is the inscription. It runs over four lines and is fairly uniformly carved, with a mostly balanced and centred arrangement. Some letters have faded on the left-hand side, but they all remain legible.

Inscription	Expanded Text
DIS MANIBVS FLAVINVS	*Dis Manibus Flavinus*
EQ ALAE PETR SIGNIFER	*eques alae Petrianae signifer*
TVRCANDIDI ANXXV	*turma Candidi annorum XXV*
STIP VII H S	*stipendiorum VII hic situs*

Translation
TO THE SPIRITS OF THE DEAD
Flavinus, horseman in the Petriana cavalry wing, standard-bearer
from the troop of Candidus
25 years old with 7 years' service
buried here

Flavinus is identified by one name only, rather than the *tria nomina* of a Roman citizen, which is written in full rather than abbreviated. This tells us that he was not himself a citizen yet, though he would have earned his Roman citizenship for himself and his own family had he fulfilled his twenty-five years' service as an auxiliary soldier. Flavinus is a typically Roman name, however, suggesting he has come from a well-connected – and likely Romanised – family. We are told that he passed away at the young age of 25, and that at the time of his death he had already completed seven years in the army, meaning he was 18 years old when he began his service.

The inscription states that Flavinus was serving as an *eques* in the *Ala Petriana*, the Petrian cavalry wing. These cavalry units were often named after their commanders: in this case, Titus Pomponius Petra. The identification of Flavinus' cavalry unit on his tombstone tells us a little bit more about his origins, as the *Ala Petriana* came from Gaul – drawn from the different Gallic tribes who had been defeated by the Romans during the wars of the first century BC. The unit was stationed in Germania for a period before being sent onwards to Britannia, where they seem to have headed north towards Coria and then west towards Luguvalium and Uxelodunum (Carlisle).

Lead seals and a tombstone fragment have been found at Uxelodunum bearing the unit's name, while part of a damaged dedicatory slab naming the unit and its prefect was also recovered from Luguvalium (central Carlisle).[49] There are other hints of the unit's northern presence: a now lost fragmentary tombstone to a veteran of the *Ala Petriana* was found not far from Uxelodunum, at Voreda (Old Penrith).[50] And wooden tablets recovered from Vindolanda, a fort and settlement that lie just a mile south of Hadrian's Wall on the Stanegate road preserve personal letters written to individuals stationed there from a man called Cluvius Florus, who is identified as a decurion in the *Ala Petriana*.

On Flavinus' inscription, the lack of titles alongside the name of his unit suggests that the tombstone was erected during the Flavian period (AD 69–96). This would place Flavinus at the earliest occupation of the area at Red House Farm, which lies less than 1 mile west of Corbridge, from AD 77 until around AD 86. Or he may have been at the first fort on the Coria site from around AD 86 onwards. It is unlikely he was there after AD 98, as military diplomas show that this is the year the unit became *civium Romanorum*. This meant that the serving soldiers had been granted Roman citizenship at a certain point, and Flavinus would certainly have wanted this commemorated on his otherwise highly Romanised tombstone. By AD 122, his unit had also doubled in size, raising the number of men from around 500 to 1,000.[51] This earned it the additional title *miliariae*, from the Latin word *mille*, meaning 1,000. Given neither of these honours are included in the unit's name on the tombstone, it seems reasonable to assume that Flavinus had died before they were awarded. This earlier date for Flavinus' tombstone is also supported by the full unabbreviated form of *Dis Manibus* appearing on the inscription, which was the epigraphic custom in the Flavian period until around AD 117.

In addition to being an *eques*, the inscription tells us that Flavinus was also a standard-bearer (*signifer*) for his unit. This was an important and honourable role, which carried additional duties as well as additional pay. His primary task was carrying his unit's standard (*signum*) into battle: this was not a duty to be taken lightly, for the *signum* was not only a useful military item but also a sacred object. It held religious and ceremonial importance, and in the forts, the standards were kept in a special shrine within the headquarters building (*principia*) when not in use. The loss of a standard during battle would bring great dishonour upon the unit – not to mention it would also be considered a severely bad omen.

The imagery on the tombstone is clearly of the *Reiter* or victorious rider type, and the arrangement is fairly standard: we see Flavinus riding on horseback, facing right, rearing over the defeated enemy who is curled up beneath the horse's raised front legs. The carving work is professional and detailed, allowing for some scaling when it comes to the horse – an ongoing challenge for the ancient artist, whether working on pottery or stone, was how to include all the figures needed for any one scene without having some extend beyond the confines of the framing or without losing focus on the main character. Here, for example, if the horse was kept to scale, either its head and legs would extend beyond the frame or Flavinus would, by necessity, become smaller.

Flavinus is dressed in typical attire for an *eques*: the sleeves of his tunic can be seen gathered around his elbow and the folds drape around his upper thigh. With its original paint, the tombstone would likely have also shown the ring mail armour that he would have worn for protection over the tunic.

Underneath the tunic, he wears light trousers, which come just past his knee. On his feet he wears either soft boots with greaves or well-tied sandals: the worn stone and position of the leg make it difficult to identify either way, though boots would be the more sensible option, especially in Britannia. Flavinus may also be wearing a torc, a large decorative metal ring that sits closely around the neck. This indicates his status among his Gallic compatriots and links to the unit's other later honorifics, *torquata* ('decorated with the torc') and *bis torquata* ('twice decorated with the torc').

A sheathed sword hangs from his belt on the right side and, though now faint, you can just about still make out the oval shape of the large shield he holds on his left side (the top of which extends out behind his head). Flavinus also wears an impressive plumed helmet, the feathers caught in motion as he charges forward on horseback. The helmet would also have likely been highly decorated: several examples survive from across Britannia that show patterned domes, detailed mythological scenes on the cheek pieces, or even additional face plates for riders. Flavinus' horse is similarly well attired for battle, with a good saddle and elaborate decorated harnesses including a bridle.

Fig 2.2 Tombstone of Flavinus the *eques*, on display in Hexham Abbey.

In his left hand, Flavinus holds the standard of his unit, matching the inscription's mention of his additional role as a standard-bearer. The *signifer* of the auxiliary cavalry wings (*alae*) most often carried a standard called the *vexillum*, which was comprised of a square piece of fabric hung from a crossbar on a spear or pole. The square fabric declared the unit's name, number and titles and could also be decorated with the unit's imagery. But here on the tombstone, you can see Flavinus holds a slightly different kind of standard. It is still in the shape of a spear but instead features a large circle towards the top. Inside the circle is a portrait, the head of which is surrounded by a radiate crown. This imagery is associated with the sun god Sol, a popular god with soldiers in the army who appears on many altars and stone reliefs in Britannia, as well as on Roman coins. On the standard, this could be the god himself or it could be a portrait of the current emperor with the god's attributes. The very top of the standard is now lost but you can still just about make out feathery remnants of the eagle that would have originally sat on top. Perhaps the stonemason who carved the relief was more accustomed to carving this type of standard – or simply thought it was more aesthetically pleasing for the rider to carry on his memorial.

The other figure on the tombstone is the defeated enemy. He is shown as the typical Roman trope of a 'barbarian' – that is to say, a non-Roman – with wild hair and beard, no armour and no clothing. He lies prostrate on the ground beneath the horse, his head turned upwards towards Flavinus, still holding his short sword and oval shield in his hands.

The stonemason has provided an unambiguous picture of Flavinus' military success, showing the point at which he kicks the defeated enemy when he is, quite literally, down – his foot eternally captured in a moment of sharp contact with the man's backside. It is a Roman triumph – and for Flavinus, as a Gaul without Roman citizenship, it is a clear statement of his allegiance and Romanisation. For, in reality, what truly separates him from the barbarian he rides over?

LUCIUS VITELLIUS TANCINUS
VETTONES CAVALRY WING

Many large tombstones from the Roman era were broken up for use in later construction. Distributed across different sites, these fragments leave behind a puzzle for archaeologists and historians to reassemble – if they are found. Take, for example, the tombstone of Lucius Vitellius Tancinus in Aquae Sulis (Bath). One of the earliest descriptions and illustrations of the tombstone comes from Collinson's 1791 work *The History and Antiquities of the County of Somerset*. He notes that before 1736, a fragment of this stone could be seen fixed onto the wall in the eastern end of the Abbey in Bath. According to his description, this fragment showed 'the figure of an equestrian soldier, armed with his spear, and trampling on his fallen enemy'.[52] Only the upper left corner of the inscription was preserved along with it, making it especially difficult to gain any further information about its original function and identity. Then, in August 1736, the tombstone's lower section with the remainder of the inscription was recovered during work to dig a vault near the old marketplace. It had been used in the foundations in a house. Reunited, these two fragments completed the inscription, and restored the name of the tombstone's subject – Lucius Vitellius Tancinus – along with key information about his military career in the auxiliary forces.

Inscription	**Expanded Text**
L VITELLIVS MA	*Lucius Vitellius*
NTAI F TANCINVS	*Mantai filius Tancinus*
CIVES HISP CAVRIESIS	*cives Hispanus Cauriensis*
EQ ALAE VETTONVMCR	*eques alae Vettonum civium Romanorum*
ANN XXXXVI STIP XXVI	*annorum XXXXVI stipendiorum XXVI*
H S E	*hic situs est*

Translation

Lucius Vitellius Tancinus
son of Mantaius, citizen of Caurium in Hispania
horseman of the Vettones Civium
Romanorum cavalry wing
46 years old with 26 years' service
HERE HE LIES

The inscription sits within a recessed rectangular panel and is uniformly spaced; the top line with the deceased's name is carved in a slightly larger size than the rest, and the stonemason has added small leaves as interpuncts. This time our horseman has been identified through the full *tria nomina* of a Roman citizen: Lucius Vitellius Tancinus. The initial L at the beginning of the inscription is the standard abbreviation for the common Roman praenomen Lucius, while his nomen (Vitellius) and cognomen (Tancinus) are written in full. Between the nomen and cognomen we find his filiation – MANTAI F – which identifies him as the son (F = *filius*) of Mantaius (Mantai/Mantaii is the genitive form of the noun, meaning 'of Mantaius'). Mantaius was not a Roman citizen, and Tancinus has noticeably not carried forward his father's name as part of his own.

We are told that Tancinus is originally from Caurium in the Roman province of Lusitania (modern-day Coria in western Spain), and indeed the name Tancinus appears on other inscriptions in this region. He was a horseman in the Vettones cavalry wing: this unit of around 500 men was drawn from the Vettones population, a cluster of tribes across the Tagus valley in the west of Spain. The letters C R after the unit's name indicate that the men had been awarded Roman citizenship (*civium Romanorum*) for their service, possibly as a result of their involvement in the emperor Claudius' invasion of Britain, which began in AD 43. This period would also point to the source of Tancinus' new Roman praenomen and cognomen: the Roman politician Lucius Vitellius, a close friend of the emperor Claudius, who served as consul with him in the years AD 43 and AD 47, then as joint censor with the emperor in the years AD 47–48.[53] It seems likely that Tancinus' tombstone dates from the first century AD, either during the final years of Claudius' imperial rule or during the early days of his successor Nero's reign.

Fig 2.3 Tombstone of Lucius Vitellius Tancinus, on display at the Roman Baths museum, Bath.

Tancinus himself passed away at the age of 46. He had served in the army for twenty-six years at the time of his death, and must have been a formidable horseman to have enjoyed such a comparatively long career. Perhaps, as some have suggested, he had ventured to Aquae Sulis to find relief from an illness or injury at the healing springs. Although only a partial section of Tancinus' tombstone survives and is rather worn away on the surface, it is another clear example of the victorious rider scene. In the relief, the horse and rider are depicted facing right, the horse's front legs are raised, and an enemy lies prostrate on the ground underneath. This time, the enemy lies further under the horse on his back, as if the image was captured at the very moment of defeat. He still wields his sword, thrusting it upwards towards the horse in the hope of striking a final blow. As on Flavinus' tombstone, the rider seems to make contact with the enemy with his right leg, perhaps having kicked away his shield. Here, too, the added detail of the horse's rear legs descending on the enemy make clear he is about to be trampled underfoot.

In his 1791 record of the tombstone, Collinson had provided an illustration in which the diagonal fracture line can be seen cutting through the top left of the inscription, separating the middle and lower sections.

There is also another fracture line running horizontally across the body of the horse, which corresponds to the Abbey fragment's condition: indeed, when in place at the Abbey, the Reverend Scarth in his own 1852 work, *On the Roman Remains Discovered in Bath*, had noted that the stone showed only the lower legs of the rider, the horse's body and legs, and the trampled enemy. So where did the

Fig. 2.4 Collinson's illustration of Tancinus' tombstone, with added third (top) fragment.

Fig. 2.5 Grosvenor Gardens 'Rider' fragment, on display at the Roman Baths museum, Bath.

top section come from in Collinson's illustration? The source is actually a fragment of another victorious rider scene, which had already been discovered in Bath in 1714 in the Grosvenor Gardens area.

It is the upper part of a gabled tombstone that featured a rider, facing to the right, wielding a spear. The stone has been broken on a horizontal line, just under the horse's head. There was much hope that this fragment could be the lost upper section of Lucius Vitellius Tancinus' tombstone, but when all fragments were brought together the scale and design of the Grosvenor Gardens piece did not match. The two reunited sections of Lucius Vitellius Tancinus' tombstone can now be seen on display in the city's Roman Baths museum, along with the Grosvenor Gardens fragment.

INSUS, SON OF VODULLUS
AUGUSTA CAVALRY WING

During excavations in Lancaster in 2005, archaeologists recovered a large millstone grit tombstone close to the Roman road that led out of the fort.[54] Although the tombstone had been damaged, it was able to be reconstructed almost in full. Measuring well over 2 metres tall, the gabled monument features a detailed relief of the victorious rider scene with four lines of inscription underneath. The relief takes up almost the entire monument and has survived in good condition despite the main fracture that separated the rider's head from the rest of his body. The inscription at the bottom is simple but mostly legible, although a couple of letters have been lost on each side. There were still traces of vermillion paint on the letters when discovered.

<table>
<tr><td align="center">Inscription</td><td align="center">Expanded Text</td></tr>
<tr><td align="center">DIS</td><td align="center">Dis Manibus</td></tr>
<tr><td align="center">MANIBVS INSVS VODVLLI</td><td align="center">Insus Vodulli</td></tr>
<tr><td align="center">[...] IVS CIVE TREVER EQVES ALAE AVG</td><td align="center">[fil] ius cives Trever eques alae Augusti</td></tr>
<tr><td align="center">[T] VICTORIS CVRATOR DOMITIA [...]</td><td align="center">[turma] Victoris curator Domitia [...]</td></tr>
</table>

Translation
TO THE SPIRITS OF THE DEAD
Insus, son of Vodullus,
citizen of the Treveri
horseman of the Augusta cavalry wing
curator in the [troop] of Victor. Domitia [set this up]

The execution of the inscription is a little haphazard compared to some of the others we've seen so far. The top line contains only the word *Dis*, with *Manibus* separated onto the second line: this is an unusual separation for the standard invocation, especially when written in full. The off-centre alignment of the word *Dis* suggests that the stonemason had originally intended to carve both words on the first line but miscalculated his space and ran out of room, having to relegate *Manibus* to the next line down.

The use of *Dis Manibus* here is helpful for narrowing the date range of the tombstone. As we've seen already, writing the full unabbreviated form on tombstones was the common epigraphic habit from the Flavian period (AD 69–96) until around the Trajanic period (AD 98–117) when the abbreviated D M became more popular. The fort at Lancaster was built during its conquest in the early AD 70s, and records tell us that the *Ala Augusta* was stationed there until the end of the second century. It is then found up at Cilurnum (Chesters) on Hadrian's Wall in AD 140, and Maglona (Old Carlisle) in AD 180. Taking all that into account, the tombstone for Insus was likely erected either towards the end of the first century or within the first couple of decades of the second.

The epitaph provides us with the name of the deceased: Insus. He is identified by only one name, along with his filiation, son of Vodullus. The single names indicate that neither of these men were Roman citizens, and indeed the tombstone clarifies that Insus' origins lie with the Treveri people. The Treveri were part of the Belgae cluster of tribes. They were based in the south-western area of modern-day Germany, with a central settlement in Colonia Augusta Treverorum (Trier). The Treveri had a long reputation of military ferocity and cavalry expertise; Caesar himself had used them as auxiliary forces in his expeditions against the Gauls, and described their reputation for excellence in battle as unparalleled among the Gauls.[55]

Within his auxiliary cavalry wing, he belonged to the subunit (*turma*) of Victor. We're also told that Insus held an additional role within his unit: he was the curator. This is an especially useful piece of information as it tells us a little bit more about Insus himself. The curator was responsible for looking after the provisions for his *turma*, including food and fodder for the horses. This not only means that Insus must have had a good level of numeracy, but also – and perhaps more importantly, for a soldier – that he was trusted by his comrades.

Unusually for a military tombstone, we are not told what age Insus was at the time of death, nor how many years of service he had completed with the army. The only other information provided is that a woman named Domitia has erected the monument for him – the gap after her name potentially once containing the abbreviation F (*fecit* – 'made this') or F C (*faciendum curavit* – 'took care to set this up') to indicate that his memorialisation through this imposing monument was her responsibility. Domitia could be a female relative or Insus' *de facto* wife. While soldiers were not permitted to legally marry during their service, in reality many had partners and families.

By far the most striking part of Insus' tombstone is the relief. It is well carved and detailed, set within a decorative gabled recess. At the apex is a gorgon head with snaked hair emanating from the top of her head. This is not as unusual as it may sound: the gorgon head (sometimes referred to as a *gorgoneion*) was often used on ancient art as a symbol of protection. The gorgon head was also linked closely with Minerva, the goddess of war, who wore it on her chest and carried it on her shield. Snake-like 'S' shapes descend on both sides of the gable border, ending with a cluster of oak leaves on each side. Oak leaves held particular significance in Roman military symbolism as they were used in the *corona civica*, a military honour awarded to someone who had saved the life of a Roman citizen in battle. Although Insus is not wearing the crown here, and only the scattered leaves are shown, it may well still allude to his strength and skill in battle.

The overall scene has the clear components of a victorious rider type: a well-dressed soldier – presumably representing Insus – seated on horseback gazes down at the viewer as his horse rears over a defeated enemy. Insus is dressed in a long-sleeved tunic, trousers and boots. A thick cloak, fastened with a rosette brooch, billows out behind him as he rides forwards. Like Flavinus, he wears an impressive plumed helmet complete with cheekpieces. He holds a weapon in the right hand and raises an oval shield with his left. His horse is similarly well equipped with fringed saddlecloth, bridle and reins. It also shows off a neatly plaited mane and tail.

Yet there is one noticeable departure from the traditional scenes: the decapitated head swinging from Insus' right hand. This is unparalleled on other funerary rider scenes and may well be an example of Insus' own heritage merging with his Roman presentation. As we have seen already with the tombstone of Aurelius Lucius above, headhunting was a tradition associated with Celtic warriors, and though Insus may have joined the Roman army, he has evidently remained proud of his roots with the fiercely brave Treveri. In the scene, Insus wields a short sword (*gladius*), also in his right hand, which is a rather unusual choice for an *eques*. Usually, these soldiers were depicted with spears, javelins or long swords – weapons that would be much more useful to anyone on horseback. But here our stonemason has opted for the *gladius*, emphasising Insus' skills with a weapon as well as his daring – he would have to get fairly close to his opponent to be able to inflict such gruesome damage.

The tombstone of Insus has, understandably, caused quite the stir since its discovery. There are many great resources for discovering more about his life and career, including the short dedicated book *Triumphant Rider: The Lancaster Roman Cavalry Tombstone* by Stephen Bull. And of course, you can visit Insus yourself, as he remains on display in Lancaster City Museum, glaring out at visitors from across the centuries.

CRESCENS THE BODYGUARD
SEBOSIANA CAVALRY WING

In 2007, a fragmentary Roman tombstone was discovered among debris from a ploughed field in Carberry, near Inveresk in Scotland.[56] Lying within the strategic territory between Hadrian's Wall and the Antonine Wall, Inveresk was home to a large Roman auxiliary fort and civilian settlement (*vicus*). The fort was likely built during the Antonine occupation and abandoned around AD 160, when Hadrian's Wall was refortified and once more became the boundary of the northern frontier. Early archaeologists had speculated that the fort was home to a cavalry unit. Although excavations had taken place across the Inveresk site during the twentieth century, this 2007 discovery was widely reported in the news, as it was the first Roman tombstone to be found in Scotland for 170 years.

The upper section of the red sandstone tombstone does not survive, but there are some remnants of the original scene still visible – a defeated enemy on the ground, a horse's hoof and a rider's foot – which tell us the lost relief was indeed the victorious rider scene. The surviving lower part of the stone features an inscription within a recessed ansate panel. The stone has evidently been reused at some point and is well worn, with a large cut through part of the inscription. The lettering is thankfully still visible and records that the monument was erected for an *eques* called Crescens.

Inscription	Expanded Text
D M	*Dis Manibus*
CRESCENTIS EQ	*Crescentis equitis*
ALAE SEBOSIA	*alae Sebosiane*
EX N EQ SING	*ex numero equitium singularium*
STIP XV	*stipendiorum XV*
H F C	*heres faciendum curavit*

Translation
TO THE SPIRITS OF THE DEAD
For Crescens, horseman
of the Sebosiana cavalry wing,
a member of the *Equites Singulares*
with 25 years' service
his heir had this set up

Unlike Insus above, we do not have the unabbreviated dedication to the Manes at the beginning of the inscription: instead, we find the abbreviation D M for *Dis Manibus* – something we shall see much more of in the tombstones that follow. His name is given in the dative case (hence it appears as *Crescentis*), which tells us this monument was erected *to* or *for* Crescens. Once again, we have only a single name provided, indicating that Crescens was not a Roman citizen. There is no filiation given though the rest of the inscription contains most of the typical information expected on a military tombstone: his name, his unit and his length of service.

Crescens is identified as an *eques* belonging to the Sebosiana cavalry wing. The Sebosiana was a unit originally from Gaul, and had been stationed in Germania Superior and then briefly in Italy before being sent to Britannia in the early AD 70s. It appears to have first been stationed at Luguvalium. Later inscriptions show that it was then in Verteris (Brough-under-Stainmore in Cumbria), and involved in restoration work to the baths in Lancaster in AD 262–266. A prefect of the *Ala Sebosiana* erected an altar on a hunting trip out near Vinovia (Binchester) fort to celebrate his successful capture of a boar that had eluded his comrades. The unit is also mentioned in the Vindolanda letters.

Like Flavinus and Insus, the inscription tells us Crescens also holds an additional role alongside *eques*. He is described as one of the *equites singulares*: these were mounted bodyguards who, out in Britannia, would have protected the provincial governor as he carried out his duties. Crescens would have been seconded to this unit to perform this duty full time, though he still kept his affiliation with the *Ala Sebosiana* as his 'home' unit. Given their roles, most evidence for *equites singulares* is found in provincial capitals. So how has Crescens ended up in the far north of the province instead? There are several intriguing theories suggested on the *Roman Inscriptions of Britain* database entry for the stone: the most likely seems to be that Crescens passed away while accompanying the governor or another Roman official on a visit to the northern frontier. Indeed, altars dedicated by the procurator Quintus Lusius Sabinianus were previously discovered at the site in Inveresk, indicating it was a destination for visiting officials during the Antonine period. Perhaps Quintus Lusius Sabinianus was even the man Crescens was tasked with protecting when he met his unfortunate end.

We are told his number of years' service to the army (here abbreviated to STIP plus numerals), which for Crescens amounts to twenty-five years in total. This is an impressive career, and one that would have earned him the opportunity to retire and be awarded with Roman citizenship for himself and his family. We are not given an age at the time of death, though given the number of years' service, Crescens may well have been in his forties or even fifties depending on the age at which he joined the army.

Fig. 2.6 Fragmentary tombstone of a *draconarius*, on display at the Grosvenor Museum, Chester.

The standard abbreviation H F C at the end tells us his heir was responsible for erecting the monument, though they are not named.

As noted, the full relief panel has unfortunately not survived. Only the figure of the enemy (possibly naked) is still visible: having fallen backwards to the ground, he presumably looks up at the horseback adversary who advances upon him. The rear hoof of the horse and part of the rider's foot can just about be identified. Crescens' commemoration is thus no doubt another example of the victorious rider, emphasising his own lengthy and successful career as both an *eques* and specialist mounted bodyguard.

THE DRACONARIUS

While the victorious rider scene is a popular choice for the *eques*, it is not the only depiction of the military horseman that we find on tombstones. A great example has been preserved on the upper sections of a fragmented tombstone from Deva, discovered recycled in the north wall.

In this case, no inscription has survived to help with identification. But there are some clues in the imagery itself. You can see that the rider wears a distinctive conical helmet and holds an object up in his left hand. The object itself does not survive clearly on the damaged stone, but it is possible to see its long serpent-like tail, which streams out behind him as he rides. This is a specific type of cavalry standard known as a *draco*, the Latin word for a serpent or dragon. It consisted of a hollow bronze dragon head mounted on a pole: the jaws and back of the head were open, and a long fabric tube was attached to the back. When carried at speed on horseback, wind passed through the head and tube, creating an eerie shrieking noise. The soldier responsible for carrying this type of standard was known as the *draconarius*. These standards were introduced to the Roman army in the second century AD: before that, they were associated with ancient nomadic peoples, especially the Dacians. The *draco* is shown carried by Dacian soldiers in scenes of the Dacian Wars from Trajan's Column in Rome.

There has been much debate about the nationality of the rider shown here: while the *draco* was closely linked with the Dacians, the rider himself is dressed in the tall conical hat of the Sarmatians rather than the soft Phrygian cap of the Dacians, and carries a short sword rather than the curved Dacian sword. The Sarmatians were a nomadic people from the plains between the Black Sea and the Caspian Sea, who moved gradually west, and indeed strategically supported the Dacians in their wars against the Roman Empire. The First Aelian Cohort of Dacians (Cohors I Aelia Dacorum) was stationed in the north of Britannia not long after the annexation of Dacia as a Roman province in the second century AD. The unit was sent north to Hadrian's Wall, where it seems to have remained for almost 300 years, but there is no evidence it had a cavalry wing.

Without an inscription it is impossible to definitively assign an origin to our *draconarius* or discover a reason for his presence at Deva. But he nonetheless provides a useful insight into the diversity of roles within the army, as well as the diversity of soldiers stationed in Britannia who often chose to be memorialised in a way that honoured their own heritage, too.

THE IMAGINIFER

Of course, not all standard-bearers in the army were mounted. Another fragmentary tombstone from Deva shows the partial figure of an *imaginifer*, a standard-bearer, fully dressed in military attire and still holding his standard.[57]

This stone, like many others, was recycled in the building of Chester's walls: the top section is now lost, leaving only the body of the figure from the neck down. The other end of the stone has unfortunately not fared much better, and only a handful of letters from the inscription remain.

<table>
<tr><td align="center">Inscription
D M
AV[..] LIVS DIOGEN[..]
[...] GINIFER
[...]</td><td align="center">Expanded Text
Dis Manibus
Aurelius Diogenes
imaginifer
[...]</td></tr>
</table>

Translation
TO THE SPIRITS OF THE DEAD
Aurelius Diogenes
standard-bearer
[...]

The initial invocation is abbreviated to the standard D M (*Dis Manibus*) and uniformly spaced across the first line. This is followed by the name of the deceased, Aurelius Diogenes. The remaining letters in the second line tell us that within the army he was an *imaginifer*, a standard-bearer. We have no further information about his unit, his age at the time of death, or his length of service.

While Aurelius is a standard Roman nomen, Diogenes is a Greek name. The practice of writing two names for Roman citizens rather than the full *tria nomina* became more prevalent from the third century AD onwards — and given that the *imaginifer* was a position only attested in legions and praetorian cohorts, not in auxiliary forces, we can be rather more certain

Fig. 2.7 Tombstone of Aurelius Diogenes, on display at the Grosvenor Museum, Chester.

in this case that he was in fact a Roman citizen, albeit one with Greek origins.[58] It is likely that he belonged to the Twentieth Legion (Valeria Victrix), which was stationed at Deva from AD 88 until at least the end of the third century.

Being responsible for the standards of the military unit was a significant undertaking: as discussed already with Flavinus' tombstone above, the standard (*signum*) was a sacred military object and its loss during battle would bring enormous dishonour to the troops within the unit. As *imaginifer*, Diogenes was responsible for carrying the *imago*, a standard that featured the portrait of the reigning emperor. This was usually made from sheet metal, which was hammered into shape by craftsmen. This imposing symbol of imperial authority on the battlefield would have reminded the soldiers of their duty and unified them in their mission on behalf of the empire.

Because of the damage to the tombstone, there is little else to be read from the inscription, but the relief provides a snapshot of the *imaginifer* on duty. Diogenes is dressed in sensible warm clothing for Britannia: he wears a long thick tunic covered by a cloak (*sagum*) that hangs down over his chest and almost to his knees in long triangular folds. He draws his cloak closed at the front with his left hand. In his right hand he holds the standard: the bust of the emperor is still visible in outline though the details have been lost. The portrait is fixed to a wooden pole, and towards the bottom of it, the handles that Diogenes would have used to raise and carry the standard can still be clearly seen.

THE SIGNIFER

An impressive limestone tombstone from Eboracum (York) captures another standard-bearer on duty for all eternity. Measuring almost 2 metres tall, the stone has survived almost in full, though the lower part is missing below the inscription and there has been some deliberate damage to the face. It was discovered in 1686 in the Micklegate area, on the site of the Holy Trinity Priory. Occupying about two thirds of the stone is the large full-body relief of a soldier, standing within a recessed niche. He is dressed in more casual military attire than some of our other soldiers and carries the standard (*signum*) of his unit. Beneath the relief is a simple moulded panel containing the inscription. Although the lower frame of the panel is missing, the epitaph itself is fortunately preserved in full.

<table>
<tr><td>Inscription</td><td>Expanded Text</td></tr>
<tr><td>L DVCCIVS</td><td>Lucius Duccius</td></tr>
<tr><td>L VOLT RVFI</td><td>Luci (filius) Voltinia Rufinus</td></tr>
<tr><td>NVS VIEN</td><td>Vienna</td></tr>
<tr><td>SIGNIF LEG VIIII</td><td>signifer legionis VIIII</td></tr>
<tr><td>AN XX IIX</td><td>annorum XXIIX</td></tr>
<tr><td>H S E</td><td>hic situs est</td></tr>
</table>

Translation
Lucius Duccius Rufinus
son of Lucius, of the Voltinian voting tribe,
from Vienna
standard-bearer of the Ninth Legion
28 years old
HERE HE LIES

The lettering is spaced over six lines, and there are small triangular interpuncts between words. There are a couple of ligatures within the text for LT (second line) and NIF (fourth line). The epitaph does not have the invocation to the spirits of the dead, possibly indicating an earlier date in the first century AD. The inscription records the soldier's name, including his filiation and voting tribe, along with his unit, role, and age at time of death. It ends with the standard funerary formula H S E, denoting the tombstone as a marker for the deceased's body or cremated remains.

The deceased is named as Lucius Duccius Rufinus, the formal *tria nomina* of a Roman citizen. You can see on the inscription that Lucius is not written in full but simply known from the letter L: as there was only a set range of male praenomen to choose from, abbreviation was an easy and helpful way to record them on inscriptions. Rufinus belongs to the Voltinian voting tribe (*tribus*), which was, during the imperial period, often where citizens from Gallia Narbonensis were placed. And indeed, Rufinus is identified as hailing from Vienna (modern-day Vienne in the south of France, not to be confused with the Austrian Vienna), a city in that region which had received the rank of *colonia* under the emperor Augustus. This bestowed citizenship on all inhabitants.

Rufinus is a standard-bearer (*signifer*) in the Ninth Legion – *Legio IX*, though written here as VIIII. This legion was also known as *Legio IX Hispana*. It was sent to Britannia from the time of Claudius' invasion in AD 43 and moved northwards over the next few years, setting up camps in the province before founding a legionary fortress in Lindum (Lincoln). As noted above, the legion moved on to Eboracum in AD 71. They are next mentioned as part of the campaigns further north, including the Battle of Mons Graupius in AD 83, though they do not seem to have been actively involved in the conflict themselves. The last clear record of the legion in Britannia comes from a monumental inscription back once again in Eboracum, stating that they had rebuilt the south-eastern gate of the legionary fort there between December AD 107 and December AD 108.[59] The sixth legion (*Legio VI Victrix*) then replaced the ninth at Eboracum in AD 122, and little secure record can be found of the latter after this – leading to intense speculation about their fate. Were they wiped out by the Brigantes during an attack on Eboracum? Or lost in the wilds of the far north on another Scottish campaign? Or were they simply sent on to another province, where they suffered a similarly serious defeat? Whatever the answer – and opinion certainly varies! – the Ninth Legion is not included in the list of thirty-three active legions inscribed on the 'Colonnetta Maffei' stone from the city of Rome, thought to date from the reign of Marcus Aurelius (AD 161–180).

Fig. 2.8 Tombstone of Lucius Duccius Rufinus, on display at the Yorkshire Museum, York.

What does this all mean for our standard-bearer Rufinus? We can, at least, give his tombstone a date range between AD 71 and 122 at the very broadest. At some point during this period, Rufinus passed away, at the age of 28. We are not told how many years he spent with the Ninth Legion, but the impressive monument left in his memory is at least evidence of his dutiful service as *signifer*.

On the tombstone itself, Rufinus is shown standing within a recessed niche, directly facing the viewer. He is dressed in military clothing suitable for life in the province: a long-sleeved tunic and a heavy cloak, which drapes down to his knees in a pointed 'V' shape. This is again an example of a *paenula*, a hooded travel cloak made from one large piece of coarse wool or felt. It could be worn over the head (like a poncho) or gathered around the shoulders and fastened with a brooch. Rufinus' hair is short and tidy. Because of the damage to his face, little more of his features can be discerned.

In his right hand, Rufinus holds the military standard for his century. You can see it is different to the standards we have encountered on some of the other tombstones so far: this time, it is a long pole decorated with four circular medallions and topped with a human hand (*manus*) with palm open. It is thought this symbolised the oath of loyalty taken by the soldiers on joining the army. In his left hand he clutches an object related to his administrative duties, called a *codex ansatus*. This was a kind of carry case for wax tablets, which were used for writing and keeping records. You can see that Rufinus holds it by a small handle. He would have used this while carrying out the duties of treasurer, a secondary responsibility that came with holding the role of *signifer* within a century. This involved managing the unit's finances, including the pay of the soldiers. The depiction of the writing tablets in his hand indicates Rufinus' skill at this part of his duties, too. Visitors to the Yorkshire Museum in York can come face to face with Rufinus, as he continues to carry the standard of the mysterious Ninth Legion in their Roman galleries.

THE VEXING VEXILLARIUS

A fragmentary tombstone recovered from Coria highlights how some stones – and their inscriptions – can result in more questions than answers.[60] The buff sandstone monument had at some point been broken up and reused for paving at the site. As a result, the upper section has been lost and a small section of the inscription is missing on the left side. Luckily, given the formulaic nature of Roman epitaphs, the missing text can be reconstructed.

<table>
<tr><td>**Inscription**</td><td>**Expanded Text**</td></tr>
<tr><td>[D] M</td><td>*Dis Manibus*</td></tr>
<tr><td>[BAR] ATHES PAL</td><td>*Barathes Palmorenus*</td></tr>
<tr><td>MORENVS VEXILA</td><td>*vexillarius*</td></tr>
<tr><td>VIXIT ANOS LXVIII</td><td>*vixit annos LXVIII*</td></tr>
</table>

Translation
TO THE SPIRITS OF THE DEAD
Barathes the Palmyrene
vexillarius
he lived for 68 years

Following the abbreviated dedication to the spirits of the dead (D M), we are told that the tombstone has been set up in memory of a man called Barathes. Barathes is described as 'the Palmyrene', indicating that he has originally come from Palmyra – a long way away from the northern frontier. Palmyra was a wealthy ancient city that had come under Roman control during the reign of the emperor Tiberius as part of the province of Syria. Inscriptions from the city record its economic significance as a highly successful trading centre between east and west during the Roman Empire. Many Syrians were also recruited into the Roman army for their expertise in mounted archery; indeed, the First Cohort of Hamians (Cohorts I Hamiorum sagittariorum) was stationed in Britannia up at Magna (Carvoran) fort near Hadrian's Wall, with a brief interlude of around twenty years further up north on the Antonine Wall.[61]

What makes this particular tombstone so vexing, then? There has been much debate over how exactly to interpret the role that Barathes held, as we have so little information on the tombstone to help contextualise it. Most read the inscribed VEXILA as an abbreviation for *vexillarius*. Within the military, the *vexillarius* is a standard-bearer who carried the *vexillum* – a woven fabric flag or banner. But we do not find any of the usual information recorded for a military role here: there are no details given about his unit nor any indication of his length of service. And indeed, at the age of 68, Barathes would not be a serving soldier at the time of his death; he would surely be retired, yet he is not described as a veteran. He is also only identified by a single non-Roman name: there is no indication that he has acquired the citizenship he would have been entitled to had he retired from the army after his required length of service.

Birley proposes that Barathes was instead a flag-maker, rather than a standard-bearer, and while this is a neat solution, it would be a unique meaning of the term.[62] Other suggestions include that he was part of a wider trade diaspora, a flag-bearer in a corporation of craftsmen, a Syrian trader who accompanied the army, or even a former soldier-turned-merchant.[63] An inscription from nearby Vindolanda uses the same abbreviated term – VEXILA – to record building work carried out by a detachment (*vexillatio*) from the Twentieth Legion.[64] Could the VEXILA on Barathes' stone instead be meant to indicate he had been attached – in some way – to a military unit? Corbridge was occupied by several detachments across its history though all of them were legionary: inscriptions place detachments from the Sixth Legion and Twentieth Legion there from the AD 160s onwards, as well as from the Second Legion Augusta later in the third century. One particularly illustrative inscription identifies the presence of a detachment from the Second Legion Augusta through a carved and labelled flag (*vexillum*).[65]

Perhaps Barathes had been an archer with the nearby group of Syrians – the Cohort of Hamians at Magna fort about 20 miles west of Coria. There is certainly other evidence for the archers away from Magna, including an impressive tombstone from Vercovicium fort. While there is no record of the Hamians being stationed at Vercovicium, Birley points out that does not necessarily rule out the movement of small numbers of – or even individual – troops between these military sites.[66] Given his age, then, had Barathes perhaps retired to the bustling nearby town of Coria following a stint with the Hamian archers? These possibilities all leave us with the same problem as before: if Barathes had served in the army or been attached to a military unit in some way, it would still be unusual not to record the name of the unit and clarify his association to them alongside his identification as *vexillarius*. Thus, whether a flag-maker, standard-bearer, trader or an auxiliary soldier, the least we can likely say is that Barathes was involved with the army at some point in his long and well-travelled life.

However, this is not the only intriguing part of Barathes' story. He is also mentioned on one of the tombstones we will see in Chapter 5. This elaborate monument to a woman called Regina was erected by her husband, a man identified in the inscription as BARATES PALMYRENUS (Barates of Palmyra) in Latin, as well as in Palmyrene script. Barates/Barathes was a typical Palmyrene name, but as Tomlin notes, it would not have been especially common along this one small stretch of the Tyne Valley – further suggesting his identification as 'the Palmyrene' on both monuments is a reference to the same person.[67] This would place Barathes over at Arbeia fort, in modern-day South Shields, at some point before his death at Coria. Does that help shed any light on his own occupation? Alas, not really – some have linked him with the Tigris boatmen who were at Arbeia but the connection is only conjecture.[68] We will see more about Barathes and Regina in the discussion of her tombstone. For now, it is interesting to note the contrast between her beautifully carved bilingual memorial and Barathes' modest monument – though even on this small and simple stone, he has if nothing else preserved the layers of his identity as a Palmyrene in the Roman world, ending his days at one of the furthest edges of the empire.

Chapter 3

Men, Freedmen and Slaves

Not all the tombstones that survive from Britannia were for those who served in the military. We find many examples across the province that record the lives and deaths of men, women and children from different social classes and a wide variety of backgrounds. While women are most often commemorated for their roles as wives, mothers, daughters or sisters, we will see in the selection which follows that the options for memorialising men were much more varied. That is not to say men had fewer socio-cultural obligations when fulfilling their roles as husbands and fathers – we certainly find dutiful and well-deserving roles for men, too. The difference for men lay in the fact that these familial roles were not the only aspects of their characters or lives that would be recorded for posterity.

A PRIEST

Towards the end of the eighteenth century, a large altar-shaped tombstone was discovered by workmen in the town of Aquae Sulis (Bath).[1] It was buried about 1.5 metres below ground level, and lay about half a mile from the famous Roman baths. The uniformly cut epitaph announced that the stone once marked the final resting place of an ancient priest.

Inscription	Expanded Text
D M	*Dis Manibus*
C CALPVRNIVS	*Gaius Calpurnius*
[R] ECEPTVS SACER	*Receptus sacer-*
DOS DEAE SV	*dos deae Su-*
LIS VIX AN LXXV	*lis vixit annos LXXV*
CALPVRNIA TRIFO	*Calpurnia Trifo-*
SA LIBERT CONIUNX	*sa liberta coniunx*
F C	*faciendum curavit*

Translation
TO THE SPIRITS OF THE DEAD
Gaius Calpurnius
Receptus, priest of the
goddess Sulis
he lived 75 years
Calpurnia Trifosa
his freedwoman and wife
took care to set this up

After the customary abbreviation to the spirits of the dead (D M), we are told the name of the deceased: Gaius Calpurnius Receptus. His traditional three-part name indicates that he was a Roman citizen. Next, his occupation is recorded: he is identified as *sacerdos*, which is the Latin term for a priest. We are also told that as a priest he was in service to the goddess Sulis.

Sulis was an indigenous Celtic goddess of healing springs who had been worshipped by the Celts before the arrival of the Romans. She was the local goddess of the thermal springs in Bath – hence the Romans calling the town *Aquae Sulis*, which translates as 'the waters of Sulis'. During the Roman occupation, Sulis was merged with the Roman goddess Minerva to create the syncretised deity Sulis-Minerva. A grand classical temple to Sulis-Minerva once stood by the sacred spring and

Fig. 3.1 Tombstone of Gaius Calpurnius Receptus, on display at the Roman Baths museum, Bath.

bath complex in the town; as a priest of the goddess, Receptus would have spent much time here attending to his religious duties. Priests were not a separate caste in Roman society: they participated in social, cultural and political activities along with the other citizens.[2] They were also free to marry, as we see in the final lines of the epitaph.

Receptus lived a long life, passing away at the age of 75. The tombstone's epitaph ends by recording some information about the person who erected the monument. In this case, it was a woman called Calpurnia Trifosa, who is identified first as Receptus' freedwoman (*liberta*) and then his wife (*coniunx*). What this tells us is that Trifosa was formerly enslaved to Receptus. Her name is Greek – suggesting she herself may have originally been Greek – and means 'delicate' or 'dainty'.[3] Trifosa has then been freed at some point, taking on the new status of *liberta* as well as adding the feminine version of his nomen (Calpurnia) to her own name to acknowledge his role as her former master. Once freed, she was then married to him. This arrangement was permitted under Roman law and was not uncommon in the Roman world – we will see it again when we encounter the tombstone of another *liberta* called Regina in Chapter 4. Here it is Trifosa herself who has overseen the erection of this memorial to her husband, offering us the briefest glimpse of female agency in the Roman world. Did she compose the epitaph herself or did Receptus leave instructions for her to carry out? The only potential clue is the identification of the goddess as Sulis only – not Sulis-Minerva, her syncretised name – which could be argued as having been written by Trifosa rather than Receptus, as perhaps he would have been more likely to address the goddess by her full appellation. The choice of the altar-shaped stone is a fitting memorial for the priest: the altar was an important religious monument upon which sacrifices and offerings were given to the gods. By creating this tombstone in the form of an altar, it is almost as if Receptus' life is now gifted to the gods.

A PROVINCIAL PROCURATOR

Visitors to Room 49 of the British Museum will find a reconstructed Roman tomb that once stood in Londinium (London).[4] Grand in both its style and lettering, the monument was built to commemorate a former procurator in the province of Britannia. Pieces of the tomb were first discovered in 1852 near Tower Hill, more were uncovered in 1885 during the Inner Circle Railway construction, and even more were found in 1935 when the substation of the London Passenger Transport Board was built.[5] The tomb had been broken down and repurposed in the fortification of one of the bastions in Londinium's town wall. Given the fragmentary nature of the monumental remains there are sections of the inscribed text missing, including two full lines after his name. What is especially unusual about the deceased in this case is that we have corroborating evidence from literary sources about his life and his time in Britannia.

Inscription	**Expanded Text**
[DIS] MANIBVS	*Dis Manibus*
[C IVL C F FA] B ALPINI CLASSICIANI	*Gai Iuli Gai fili Fabia Alpini Classiciani*
[...]	*[...]*
[P] ROC PROVINC BRIT[ANNIAE]	*procuratoris proviniciae Britanniae*
IVLIA INDI FILIA PACATA I[...]	*Iulia Indi filia Pacata Indiana*
VXOR	*uxor*

Translation

TO THE SPIRITS OF THE DEAD
For Gaius Julius Alpinus Classicianus
son of Gaius, from the Fabian voting tribe
[...]
procurator for the province of Britannia
His wife, Julia Pacata Indiana, daughter of Indus,
[set this up]

This time the deceased is identified by four names: Gaius Julius Alpinus Classicianus. A second cognomen was sometimes added to record an achievement or even just as a nickname – 'Classicianus' may be derived from the Latin *classicus*, which carries the meaning of 'the highest rank' or 'superior'.[6] As part of his formal name, his filiation is noted (C F = son of Gaius), as is his voting tribe (FAB = Fabian). It is therefore of no doubt that Classicianus was a Roman citizen. Two lines are missing following his name: these likely included information on his place of origin as well as a brief career history, as we have seen on the epitaphs of military officials. Based on his own name as well as his later-named wife's known background, it has been suggested that he came from Augusta Treverorum (Trier) in Germania.[7]

The inscription picks up again after the two missing lines to record that Classicianus was procurator in the province of Britannia. This was an important position and role holders were usually drawn from the equestrian class. As a civil administrator working on behalf of the emperor, the procurator was responsible for the province's finances. This included collecting taxes and paying the soldiers who were stationed there. We know from records that Classicianus was appointed to the role in AD 61, following the Boudiccan revolt. He held the role until his death in AD 65, and so the tomb would have been created shortly after this. The historian Tacitus notes that Classicianus had succeeded Catus Decianus as procurator, but comments that he did little to instil peace with the Celtic tribes, owing to his preoccupation with ousting the governor of the province, Gaius Suetonius Paulinus.[8]

The final lines tell us that the monument was erected by his wife (*uxor*), named as Julia Pacata Indiana. She is also given her filiation as daughter of Indus (INDI FILIA), whose name can also be seen in the feminised form in her cognomen. Tacitus records that her father, Julius Indus, was a tribesman from the Treveri who helped the Romans quell a revolt from among his fellow Treveri.[9] His assembled force was then incorporated into the Roman army as the auxiliary *Ala Gallorum Indiana*, named after Indus himself, and he earned Roman citizenship for his loyalty. His auxiliary unit later came to Britannia – either with the initial invasion or as part of the reinforcements sent after the Boudiccan revolt – and was possibly stationed for a time at Corinium Dobunnorum (Cirencester).[10] As the daughter of this Treveri-tribesman-turned-Roman-ally, Julia Pacata Indiana has been able to move into the circles of Roman high society. Her name appearing on this impressive monument as the wife of Classicianus preserves her journey to the provincial ruling class of Britannia as much as his.

A BLACKSMITH

Not all tombstones survive with an epitaph intact; even so, we can still discern something about the deceased. A large gritstone monument from Eboracum (York) is a great example of this: standing at just over 1 metre tall, it features a full-figure relief of a man standing within an arched recess. We can tell he is not a soldier by the way in which he is dressed as well as from the implements in his hands – which helpfully reveal his profession as a blacksmith.

The blacksmith stands within the niche, directly facing the viewer. His face is worn but not deliberately damaged, so details of his facial features like his eyes and mouth are still discernible. He has thick curled hair cropped around the crown of his head and a full, thick beard. Unlike many of the figures we have encountered so far, the blacksmith is dressed lightly – which is certainly appropriate for his hot working environment. He wears a light short tunic with a layer of additional fabric draped over his left shoulder and around his lower torso like an apron. His arms and legs are bare, and he wears nothing on his feet.

Fig. 3.2 Tombstone of a blacksmith, on display in the Yorkshire Museum, York.

The surrounding enclosure in which the blacksmith stands is both tombstone and forge: it has decorative scrolls and rosettes around the arch yet to the viewer's left, the blacksmith interacts with an anvil that protrudes from beside the arch's supporting columns. In his left hand, he holds an object over the anvil with a pair of large tongs. This is about to be shaped with the hammer he is raising with his right hand. It is a snapshot of the deceased at work, eternally captured in the motions of his trade.

We do not have the name of the deceased or indeed any information on his life beyond his profession. The size and design of the monument nonetheless suggest a man who was successful at what he did, as this kind of tombstone would certainly not have been cheap. The decision to commemorate him hard at work – whether taken by the blacksmith himself or his family – suggests a great pride in his profession, which has ultimately become the key marker of his identity in both this life and the next.

A WELL-DESERVING SLAVE

Up along Hadrian's Wall near Onnum (Halton Chesters) fort, another fragmentary tombstone records the passing of an ancient slave.[11] It was found at Halton Castle in 1868 when work was being carried out on the stable yard. The surviving section of buff sandstone is from the lower part of the original tombstone, and measures about 0.5 metres wide by 0.5 metres tall. At least one line is missing from the inscription.

Inscription	Expanded Text
[...]	*[...]*
HARDALIO	*Hardalio-*
NIS	*nis*
COLLEGIVM	*collegium*
CONSERV	*conservorum*
B M P	*bene merenti posuit*

Translation

[...]
[for the slave/in memory] of Hardalio
the society of fellow-slaves
set this up to one who was well-deserving

The lettering on the fragment is not particularly polished but shows a certain style: the A letterforms are shaped like the Greek letter lambda and a swooping ivy leaf appears as an interpunct at the end of the second extant line. The inscription does not sit straight across the stone but is rather higgledy-piggledy. A forgotten I has been added back into the space between L and O at the end of the first line. It is not an expertly cut inscription like that of Classicianus, but there is nevertheless something characterful about its formation.

The initial lines are lost. Our epitaph starts with a name written in the genitive case. This is the case that indicates belonging – this means it may not be naming Hardalio as the deceased but rather indicating that whoever was previously named on the missing lines *belonged* to someone called Hardalio. Alternatively, it could be the case that a word such as 'memory' is missing beforehand or it is intended as indicating to whom the tombstone belongs – making this the name of the deceased after all. It is an unusual name with etymological links with an obscenity in Ancient Greek and the term 'busybody' in Latin, which would certainly be more appropriate for a slave whose name may have been picked by his master.[12]

We find out the broader identity of the deceased in the next line as we are told that the monument has been erected by a group: the *collegium conservorum*, which translates as 'society' or 'guild' of fellow-slaves. Thus, the deceased himself must have been a slave. The Romans were fond of *collegia*, organised societies that acted as legal entities for many different common-interest groups across social, political, professional, military and religious life. Many of these groups also functioned as a burial club: members would pay a regular fee to cover the cost of their later funerary expenses. This was especially important for those without close family nearby – like soldiers, merchants, veterans – or those of lesser social standing – like slaves – to ensure that they received the proper funerary rites and were commemorated with a tombstone.[13] This particular *collegium* has been set up specifically for slaves and must have been near to the deceased's location along Hadrian's Wall, which certainly would have been a rather bleak landscape to find yourself in if you were worried about who might take care of your body – and your memory – after death. The little amount of money slaves would have been able to spare may have been supplemented by donations from wealthy or benevolent patrons; the quality of the lettering suggests the work of a less expensive stonecutter.

Little other detail is given for the deceased beyond the closing abbreviation, which identifies him as well deserving. Despite his status and remote location, being a member of the burial club has ensured he received a proper – and long-lasting – commemoration after death.

A FREEDMAN

Arbeia fort in South Shields stands at the entrance to the river Tyne. These days you can still climb up to the top of the fort's reconstructed West Gate and watch the ships arriving from the North Sea. While there are more cruise liners than Roman triremes now, it is easy to see how this fort became a crucial spot for the movement of supplies – and soldiers – out across nearby Hadrian's Wall. Yet it is not only its military life that has made Arbeia well known: the cemetery there has yielded two especially notable tombstones from its former Roman inhabitants, one for a freedwoman named Regina (which we will see in Chapter 4) and the other for a freedman known as Victor.[14]

Victor's tombstone was recovered in two parts: the decorated gable was unearthed in 1881 while the rest of the monument was discovered nearby in 1885. It once stood over 1 metre tall and features a large and intricately carved portrait of the deceased enjoying a dinner party. This design occupied the majority of the stone's face; the epitaph is inscribed in a recessed panel beneath the dining scene and takes up only about a fifth of the overall space.

Inscription	**Expanded Text**
D M VICTORIS NATIONE MAVRVM	*Dis Manibus Victoris natione Maurum*
ANNORVM XX LIBERTVS NVMERIANI	*annorum XX libertus Numeriani*
EQVITIS ALA I ASTVRVM QVI	*equitis ala I asturum qui*
PIANTISSIMI PR[O SE] CVTVS EST	*piantissimi prosecutus est*

Translation
TO THE SPIRITS OF THE DEAD
For Victor, from the Moorish peoples,
20 years old. Freedman of Numerianus,
horseman in the First Wing of the Astures, who
most affectionately accompanied him to this grave.

The abbreviated invocation to the spirits of the dead does not sit on its own line but instead is immediately followed by the name of the deceased. It is written in the dative case (VICTORIS) to show that the monument is also dedicated *to* Victor himself. He is only identified by one single name, so already we may expect that he has a non-Roman background. The first line continues, and we discover that Victor has originally come from the 'Moorish' or Mauri peoples (*natione Maurum*) in Mauretania, an ancient region that spanned modern-day Algeria and northern Morocco. It had been annexed during the reign of the emperor Claudius and incorporated into the Roman Empire as two provinces. Many of the highly skilled Moorish cavalry were then recruited into the Roman auxiliary forces.[15]

At the start of the epitaph's second line, we are told that Victor passed away at the young age of 20. This is likely an estimate – a rounded number – as it is unlikely his exact age was known, given his status, which the inscription tells us next: Victor was a *libertus* – the freedman – of another man called Numerianus. Freedman was a specific category in the Roman world and indicates that Victor had previously been enslaved, likely as a child given his age at the time of death. He had then at some point earned his freedom from his master Numerianus, who erected this grand – and expensive – monument to him when he passed away. As is often the case with masters who dedicate tombstones to their freedmen and slaves, we are also given some information about Numerianus himself, which can help build more of a picture of Victor's life. Numerianus is a horseman in the cavalry wing of the Astures (*Ala I Asturum*). This auxiliary unit came to Britannia at some point in the late first century AD and was stationed at nearby Condercum fort (Benwell) on the eastern end of Hadrian's Wall. This military posting is an interesting detail as it tells us that Numerianus was not a Roman citizen either: the Astures people came from north-west Hispania and were renowned for their horses, in particular a breed called the Asturcón. This small mountain horse was recorded by the ancient geographer Pliny the Elder – who notes their smooth trot.[16] The breed still exists today.

Despite his non-Roman background, Numerianus has clearly embraced the Roman attitude to slavery: he has acquired Victor at some point during his own life (we are not told his age) and then he has completed the legal process of manumission to release him from his slavery. Given Victor's roots among the Mauri peoples, who were also famed for their excellent cavalry, some have suggested that perhaps Victor was acquired by Numerianus as a stablehand or groom for his horse.[17]

The final line of the inscription offers a glimpse into the relationship between *libertus* and former master, as Numerianus records how he accompanied Victor to his final resting place with the greatest affection. This is not exaggeration on my part as translator – the Latin word *piantissimi* written in full here is a superlative adjective, emphasising that the action was carried out with the maximum emotion possible. It is always hard to definitively identify genuine affection on an epitaph when so many of the conventions are culturally ingrained and socially expected; this is made especially difficult when the dedicator holds significant power in the relationship as former master and current patron. Was Numerianus genuinely affected by Victor's loss or was he performing the role of a caring master and patron for all to see – or was it somewhere in between? Or had they perhaps developed a closer relationship? The effusive description of Numerianus' emotional state when conducting Victor to his grave certainly aligns with the grandness of the monument's design: it is a beautiful tombstone carved in the classical style on high-quality stone which has earned the label of one of the 'most notable sculptures' to survive from the province.[18] Other monuments of this quality are dedicated by husbands to their wives, making Victor rather unique – this has led to the suggestion that it was a lover's gift, and evidences same-sex sexual relationships between masters and their freedmen or slaves.[19]

Taking a closer look at the tombstone's design, it is clear that it has been sculpted by a skilful stonemason – and possibly one with similarly far-flung origins to the two men mentioned on the inscription. There are many beautiful decorative elements to the monument, which show an affinity with the extensive funerary sculpture that survives from Palmyra (Tadmor), a thriving ancient trading city that had been incorporated within the Roman province of Syria.[20] Above the pediment are two male busts, which gaze out over the stone: both faces are now extensively damaged but the curled hair is still visible on the left bust. Both small busts wear neatly draped clothes – a toga and a cloak – and are each set within a medallion. The pediment itself features at the centre a lion's head with a ring held in its mouth (like a doorknocker); two symmetrical vines curl out to either side beneath it. Lions often appeared on ancient funerary monuments as guardians, crouching or sitting, from the Archaic period onwards. Some were even freestanding sculptures that adorned a tomb or mausoleum: indeed, even in Roman Britain we find evidence of these lions in funerary contexts. Several have been found in Corbridge in the north of England; the most famous of these – known simply as the 'Corbridge Lion' – had later been repurposed as a fountain.

Returning to Victor's tombstone, the central focus of the monument is the male figure representing the deceased himself. He is shown reclining on his left side on a very low-backed wooden couch; he leans on his left arm, his elbow resting on a cushion. The couch is furnished with a mattress, and the sculptor has taken the time to add details of the textiles that cover it, including not just the folds of the material but even its design and the fringing of the plump cushion. The wooden frame of the couch is also carved in great detail, with ornamental baluster legs and a decorative inlaid design across the base.

Victor is well dressed to match his elegant environment. He wears a loose, plain and short-sleeved tunic, which features a scalloped horizontal opening around the neck. A large rectangular cloak is draped over the tunic, falling in carefully carved folds over and around the left shoulder and arm, and again across the lower body and legs. Small tassels are visible on the edges of the cloak. He is dressed in a similar way to the men depicted on Palmyrene tombstones, though it is worth considering how the garments would have been further personalised and differentiated through the designs that would have originally been painted on top of the stone.[21] In his left hand, Victor holds a cup from which he is drinking. In his right hand, which rests on his right knee, he holds a small plant or bundle of leaves. It is similar in shape to the object held by the deceased on similar funerary banquet scenes from Palmyra, in which the central reclining figure holds a palm spray or a cluster of dates in his right hand.

Behind the reclining figure of Victor, the background of the stone is decorated with more winding vines of a plant. These fill what would otherwise have been empty space, as we see on many other Roman tombstones. The decision to include this further decoration may also point to a Palmyrene artist: while the background of tombstones there often featured portraits of other family members (as above), banqueting tesserae – small clay tokens – show this same kind of swirling vine around priests as they recline in the same position on a couch.[22]

However, Victor is not alone in his funerary banqueting scene: in front of his couch is a much smaller male figure, which represents a slave. He is shown in side profile, though the face again is now damaged, and even on this miniature figure the clothing is well detailed: he wears a short pleated and belted tunic and soft boots. The slave stands beside a large two-handled mixing bowl – which at a dinner party would contain wine and water – and holds up a filled cup. Raising it above his head with both hands, he offers it upwards towards Victor. Alongside the inscription and the beautiful monument itself, this is a clear visual testament to Victor's new status as *libertus* rather than slave: now he is the one upon whom a slave dutifully attends as he enjoys his newly gained leisure time at a dinner party.

This impressive tombstone shines a light on the movement and mixing of people at the height of the Roman Empire. Victor has originally come from

Fig. 3.3 Tombstone of Victor the freedman, on display at Arbeia fort in South Shields.

Fig. 3.4 Funerary relief from Palmyra (second to third century AD). Image courtesy of The Metropolitan Museum of Art, New York. Object Number 02.29.1.

Roman-occupied North Africa, and spent some part (if not all) of his young life enslaved. He was acquired by Numerianus, a horseman in the Asturian cavalry wing, who himself was from Hispania. Victor has accompanied Numerianus on his posting to the far north of the Romans' most northern province and they reach Arbeia fort. At some point – whether before or after their arrival in Britannia – Numerianus decides to legally release Victor from his enslavement and he takes on the status of a freedman (*libertus*), gaining a measure of freedom and rights in Roman society that he has not experienced before. Alas, while they are at Arbeia, Victor passes away at the young age of 20 or so – his rounded age likely just an estimate by Numerianus – and his bereaved patron not only takes care of his burial but also commissions this grand monument to memorialise him. And indeed, it has proved worth its initial expense: Victor's tombstone still stands at Arbeia, where he is seen and remembered by many passers-by almost 2,000 years later.

A MOST DEVOTED FATHER

A fragmentary inscription was recorded at Greta Bridge, near Barnard Castle in the north-east of England, which preserves a partial memorial for a beloved father.[23] The stone was found at some point before 1763 but has since been lost. The Romans had established an auxiliary fort in the area known as Maglona, and a small settlement (*vicus*) had developed around it. A handful of inscribed stones survived from the site including altars, building dedications and tombstones, though the latter are all now lost. An early sketch of the inscription has survived but the letterforms are difficult to ascertain at points without reference to the original stone, especially as the wider epitaph not only has some spelling errors but also employs some unusual abbreviations and ligatures.

<table>
<tr><td align="center">Inscription</td><td align="center">Expanded Text</td></tr>
<tr><td align="center">VIC[...]</td><td align="center">Vic[...]</td></tr>
<tr><td align="center">AVRELIAE ROM[ANA]</td><td align="center">Aureliae Romana et</td></tr>
<tr><td align="center">SABIN FILIE PARTI PI</td><td align="center">Sabina filiae patri pi-</td></tr>
<tr><td align="center">ENTISSIMO ET RARISSI</td><td align="center">entissimo et rarissi-</td></tr>
<tr><td align="center">MO FACNDM CVR MRI</td><td align="center">mo faciendum curaverunt [matri</td></tr>
<tr><td align="center">CAR LVI ANORR F M P A</td><td align="center">carissimae LVI annorum filiae</td></tr>
<tr><td align="center"></td><td align="center">monumentum posuit ave vale]</td></tr>
</table>

Translation
Vic[...]
Aurelia Romana and
Aurelia Sabina daughters
took care to set this up to their
most devoted and most extraordinary father
[to a dearest mother 56 years old
her daughters set up this monument, hail and farewell]

As you can see, the final line in particular is difficult to prise apart. There is a secondary inscription, starting from the three letters (MRI) which appear at the end of the penultimate line. It seems likely this is an abbreviation for *matri* ('to mother'), which could indicate an additional family member's memorialisation was also added on the same stone. But the letters that follow afterwards on the final line are poorly transcribed in the illustration, making their secure identification more difficult. One suggested reconstruction incorporates the superlative *carissimae* ('beloved' or 'dearest') plus the age of the deceased, assuming a potential typographical error in the recording of *annorum* in which the R is doubled rather than the N. It then repeats that the daughters have set up the memorial to their mother, before ending with the abbreviation A V – *ave vale*, 'hail and farewell' – which is attested elsewhere in the empire.[24] But this is ultimately all conjecture: the line could well contain the mother's name hidden within the letters instead, or another reading entirely, based on different letterforms. Fortunately, for our current investigation, we can set aside this section of the inscription, as our primary interest is in the father and his characterisation. How has he been remembered?

The name of the father is lost. The first identifiable letters to the top of the fragment – VIC – may be part of it, or it may well identify a potential military link. Although Greta Bridge was home to an auxiliary unit, one of the recovered building dedications records that a centurion from the Sixth Legion Victrix oversaw building repairs at the fort, suggesting the presence of a small legionary detachment at the turn of the third century AD.[25] On the second and third of the surviving lines we are told that the tombstone has been erected by two women, named as Aurelia Romana and Aurelia Sabina. They are identified as daughters (*filiae*) who have set up the tombstone in memory of their father (*patri*, misspelled as PARTI in the inscription). The women's shared name of Aurelia suggests that their father's nomen may have been Aurelius.

They describe him using two superlatives: most devoted (*pientissimo*) and most extraordinary (*rarissimo*), underscoring the close relationship between parent and child from the children's perspective. We will see in the next chapter how women were often characterised by their exemplarity as wives and mothers; here, though the father may well have had his own career – military or otherwise – listed previously on the epitaph, it is his utmost dedication to his role as father that is emphasised and memorialised for all to see. It is interesting that the monument has been taken care of by the two daughters, rather than a male heir or wife – though if the reading of the last section is correct then the wife had also passed away. How did these two sisters support themselves at this fairly remote military site after the death of their parents? It has been suggested that they were the daughters of the prefect there – though if he died then they would have had to vacate their living quarters – but perhaps the father, as exemplary as he was, had appointed a guardian to care for them after his death.[26]

A BORROWED SOUL

A fragment of red sandstone from Luguvalium (Carlisle) has been often interpreted as evidencing the changing beliefs in Britannia during the later years of the Roman occupation.[27] This stone was found face-down on the top of a large oak coffin during excavations to make way for new housing near Gallows Hill in 1892. Haverfield noted that the coffin contained a skull and 'fatty earth' only.[28] This site near Gallows Hill, to the south of Carlisle, runs along the London Road and was used by the Romans as a cemetery. Six lines of the inscription are preserved in full; the seventh line is damaged by the large fracture that has broken this section away from its lower part.

Inscription	**Expanded Text**
D M	*Dis Manibus*
FLAS ANTIGONVS[29] PAPIAS	*Flavius Antigonus Papias*
CIVIS GRECVS VIXIT ANNOS	*civis Grecus vixit annos*
PLVS MINVS LX QVEM AD	*plus minus LX quem ad*
MODVM ACCOMODATAM	*modum accomodatam*
FATIS ANIMAM REVOCAVIT	*fatis animam revocavit*
SEPTIMIA DOMINA [...]	*Septimia Domina [...]*

Translation
TO THE SPIRITS OF THE DEAD
Flavius Antigonus Papias
a Greek citizen lived
60 years more or less
until that time when he returned
the soul lent to him by Fate
Septimia Domina …

The lettering is clear if a little messy in execution and the guidelines remain visible throughout. The initial abbreviation to the spirits of the dead is centred on the first line but otherwise the design is fairly plain. The inscription itself is an interesting blend of style and content: we have some of the usual information like name and nationality, but we also have more poetic lines like *fatis animam revocavit*, a metrical phrase that fits into the rhythm at the end of a hexameter line.

The epitaph is dedicated to a man called Flavius Antigonus Papias. While he may have a mixed *tria nomina* of Latin and Greek names, he is described as a Greek citizen (*civis Grecus*) on the second line, leaving no uncertainty as to his nationality. What has brought this Greek citizen to the north of Britannia? The tombstone records no military links, though it offers little else by way of information on Papias' occupation. Many Greeks moved

Fig. 3.5 Tombstone of Flavius Antigonus Papias, on display at the Tullie Museum in Carlisle.

throughout the empire for trade, but the Romans also often sought to acquire Greek slaves who, on account of their cultural background, were set to work as tutors, doctors and musicians. There are a number of tombstones and altars that record the Greek men and women who had made their homes across Britannia, from Londinium to Deva Victrix and even further north, from Luguvalium to Coria.

Across the third and fourth lines, we are given some further information on his life. Papias lived for sixty years, though the inscription acknowledges this number is an estimate through the use of the phrase 'more or less' (*plus minus*). After this succession of the deceased's basic information, the epitaph then switches to the more poetic description: it records how Papias has returned the soul which had been on loan to him from fate once his allotted time (the sixty or so years) had passed. It is this sentiment – and the associated phrasing – that has provoked debate about whether or not this tombstone is Christian. Christianity had started to 'trickle into Britain' by the late second or early third century AD.[30] The Edict of Milan, which was issued by the emperors Constantine and Licinius in AD 313, granted Christians the right to religious freedom: they could now finally practise their faith without the fear of persecution. By AD 380, Theodosius had issued the Edict of Thessalonica, which established Christianity as the state religion.

Much influence came from the eastern parts of the empire, making Papias' nationality an especially interesting added detail here.[31]

On our tombstone, the invocation to the Manes as the spirits of the dead is evidently not a Christian sentiment. This would initially seem to suggest that this tombstone is following the traditional Roman polytheist tradition. Yet many Christian tombstones in Italy and the provinces more widely begin with this abbreviation.[32] By this point it had likely become funerary convention more than anything else and should not necessarily be taken as a firm indicator of religious belief; as has been argued by Woolf, the abbreviated formula could be read 'quasi-pictographically' rather than as a literal message, indicating to the viewer that the stone they observed was a monument to the dead.[33]

When used on Christian tombstones, *Dis Manibus* is often followed by a specifically Christian phrase or symbol, which instead marks out the faith of the deceased. One of these phrases is the short comment *plus minus* ('more or less'), which follows the detail of Papias' age: this appears on many Christian epitaphs and is considered in part to indicate the indifference towards the earthly body. Many – including the entry on the *Roman Inscriptions of Britain* database – consider it 'characteristically Christian'.[34] Yet it is important to note that this little phrase is found on almost 2,000 epitaphs from across the empire.[35] While it is notably common in Christian epitaphs from the fourth century AD, there are earlier examples of its use in Rome in the third century AD as well as in Africa in the second century AD.[36] Not all of these are Christian, which suggests that although the phrase may well have come to be incorporated on Christian epitaphs it was not always exclusively in use within this religious context only. Indeed, as Kruschwitz has noted, the argument that *plus minus* was a specifically Christian funerary habit has become circular as it is often used as the sole criterion for identifying an inscription as Christian.[37] Thus, the phrase as it appears here can only offer us a potential clue about Papias' religious beliefs rather than definitive proof.

Does the poetic description of Papias returning the soul that was lent to him help with the interpretation? Some read it as a Christian sentiment equivalent to the more commonly found *reddidit animam* ('he gave up his soul'), which underscores this act of resignation as a virtue.[38] The soul (*anima*) was a much-discussed topic among Roman writers, pagan and Christian. It is not surprising then that we do find it referenced occasionally on funerary inscriptions. Traditionally, in Roman religious belief, the soul was the part of the person that survived the death of the physical body. Incorporeal, it represented the very essence of the person and retained an image of their prior physical form. The idea of fate, or the personified Fates, fixing the parameters of a human lifespan was also popular in both the Ancient Greek and Roman imagination. That leaves us with another frustratingly ambiguous clue, though the collection of all of these little hints together may well support the claim that Papias was indeed a Christian after all – de la Bédoyère notes the shared name with Papias of Hierapolis, an early apostolic bishop active in Asia Minor at the turn of the second century AD.[39]

A DATE OF DEATH

While most of the Roman tombstones that survive from Britain do not follow our modern custom of recording the exact date of death on a loved one's epitaph – thus making assigning an accurate date extremely difficult – there are two noteworthy exceptions. One is a fine-grained sandstone monument from Tarrant Hinton in Dorset, which shows how the addition of even just a few seemingly simple details can allow us to precisely date someone's death. This fragmented and badly damaged stone was recovered during the excavation of a Roman villa in 1980.[40] It had originally been part of a tomb, rather than a freestanding monument. The tomb had been broken up at some point, and parts of the masonry ended up 12 metres down a filled ancient well.

Inscription
CVP VERI [F] DECESSIT
ANNO XXXVIIII
TVSCO ET BASSO COS VII KAL
SEPTEMB

Expanded Text
Cupitus Veri filius decessit
anno XXXVIIII
Tusco et Basso consulibus VII
Kalendas Septembres

Translation
Cupitus son of Verus died in his 39th year
during the consulship of Tuscus and Bassus
on 26 August AD 258

The epitaph is brief and – compared to many we've seen so far – rather blunt. Cupitus is named as the deceased and given his filiation as the son of a man called Verus. We are then told in no uncertain terms that he died (*decessit*) aged 39 years. It is the second line that provides us with the precise date for his death: we are told that it was during the consulship of two men, identified as Tuscus and Bassus. The consulship was a senior administrative role that could only be held by two men for a maximum of a year. As such, it was often used on inscriptions as a way of indicating the date, and many lists survive which record who was consul for each year. Marcus Nummius Tuscus and Mummius Bassus held the consulship together in AD 258, placing Cupitus' death in this exact year.

But we are able to pin down the date even further than that, as the inscription records that he died seven days (VII) before the Kalends of September. The Romans had their own dating system for identifying the days of the month. Instead of sequentially numbering them as we do (1st, 2nd, 3rd and so on), they referred to a specific date by how far it was from one of three fixed days in every month: the Kalends, the Nones, or the Ides. The Kalends was the first day of the month, when the moon was a thin crescent. The Nones was the fifth day of the month when the moon was quarter-full – unless it was March, May, July or October, in which case it fell on the seventh day. The Ides – the most famous of all Roman dates – fell when the moon was full. This was usually on the thirteenth of the month, unless it was March, May, July or October, in which case it fell on the fifteenth day. Therefore, in order to identify a specific date, a Roman would tell you how many days it was before the next key calendar day, counting backwards inclusively from the next of the three fixed dates. This means that 2 January would be known as *ante diem IV Nones Januarias* – four days before the Nones of January, while 30 December would be *ante diem III Kalends Januarias* – three days before the Kalends of January. Our epitaph tells us that Cupitus died *ante diem VII Kalends Septembres* – i.e. seven days before the Kalends of September. Counting backwards inclusively, this gives us a date of 26 August. Thus, we can, for this tombstone, provide Cupitus' date of death in full as 26 August AD 258. The tomb would have been erected not long after this, though we can only wonder how long it stood before it was broken up and thrown into the well as filler material.

Chapter 4

Women and Freedwomen

The surviving tombstones for women across the province can offer us a brief glimpse into their lives, though it is worth emphasising from the outset that we do not encounter the majority of these women in their own words. Their memorials are most often erected by the men they left behind, and as such their commemoration focuses on the values that society deemed essential for women to strive for in their roles as wives, daughters and mothers. Many epitaphs reference traditional virtues such as modesty (*modestia*), dutifulness (*pietas*), purity (*sanctitas*) and chastity (*castitas*). This is often matched by artistic representations that show the woman dressed in modest clothing – especially if she was a married citizen (*matrona*) – or accompanied by the tools of the industrious housewife, such as a distaff or spindle for wool working. We will also encounter many women who are memorialised with their children in the chapter that follows.

Yet even if we are viewing their funerary monuments through an idealised patriarchal lens, we can still glean an insight into the many women of different statuses, backgrounds and ethnicities who called Britannia their home. From bustling towns and cities to the windswept frontiers of Hadrian's Wall, we see how women's identities were shaped and layered as they moved across not just the province but also the wider empire.

A FAMOUS FREEDWOMAN

REGINA

One of the most well-known tombstones commemorating a woman in Roman Britain comes from Arbeia fort (South Shields) at the mouth of the river Tyne. As we discovered when looking at the tombstone of Victor in Chapter 3, Arbeia fort guarded a key access point for the transport of soldiers and supplies out across Hadrian's Wall. An extensive civilian settlement (*vicus*) developed along the road to the south of the fort and remained continuously occupied until the end of the third century.[1] In the nineteenth century, excavations and building work in an area south-west of the fort uncovered many urns with cremated remains still inside, as well as some tombstone fragments, indicating that this was the site of the cemetery.[2] Four of these fragments formed an impressive memorial to a woman called Regina, which, when restored, stood over 1 metre high and just over 0.7 metres wide.[3] There was extensive damage to the face, which had been entirely removed, but the rest of the tombstone had survived in remarkably good condition.

The majority of the monument is taken up by a detailed full-body portrait of the deceased, set within a meticulously carved ornate gabled niche. Underneath this striking portrait is an epitaph, which is just as remarkable – if not more – for being the only example of a bilingual Roman tombstone to survive from Britannia. Three lines of Latin sit within a wide rectangular panel and provide the customary information on the deceased. Beneath this, however, an additional line has been added in Palmyrene script.

Inscription	**Expanded Text**
D M REGINA LIBERTA ET CONIVGE	*Dis Manibus Regina liberta et coniuge*
BARATES PALMYRENVS NATIONE	*Barates Palmyrenus natione*
CATVALLAVNA AN XXX	*Catuallauna annorum XXX*

Translation
TO THE SPIRITS OF THE DEAD
For Regina, freedwoman and wife,
from the Catuvellaunian people
30 years old
Barates the Palmyrene (set this up)

The Latin lettering is a little haphazard, with the letterforms varying in size and shape across the three lines, though some show evident flourish and a naturally more cursive style. Interpuncts mark the spaces between the words, including at the end of the lines. Few abbreviations have been used here: only the initial dedication to the spirits of the dead (D M) and the word for years (AN) have been shortened. The Palmyrene script beneath is carved much more confidently with smooth and rounded strokes. It is a simple but effective message: 'Regina, the freedwoman of Barates, alas!'[4]

Regina is named in the first line as the deceased. She is immediately identified as a *liberta* – a freedwoman, which means that she had previously been enslaved. As we saw with the tombstone of Marcus Favonius Facilis in Chapter 2, freed slaves were no longer property but citizens with their own rights, although there were restrictions placed upon their status. Like freedmen, freedwomen remained in a legally defined position of obligation to their former master who was now known as their patron.[5] Next, the inscription also identifies her as the wife of a man called Barates, so it is likely that this was her former master who freed her in order to marry her. This was a fairly common practice, which was permitted under Roman law; the usual manumission age limits could be exempted if a male patron was freeing his slave for the purpose of marrying her himself, and the woman could be returned to slavery if she did not marry him within six months or indeed married someone else.[6] A freedwoman could take two names in the style of a freeborn Roman woman. This was usually done by adding a feminine version of her former master's name in front of her slave name; here we can see Regina retains her single (presumably slave) name only. Her given name comes directly from the Latin *regina*, meaning 'queen'.

Her husband Barates is described in the inscription as a 'Palmyrene', i.e. he was originally from Palmyra (Tadmor), a thriving ancient city that had been incorporated within the Roman province of Syria. He too is only identified with a single name, suggesting that he is a *peregrinus* – a free provincial subject – rather than a Roman citizen. There are no further details provided about Barates to know why he had come to Britannia, whether he had been in the military or was a merchant. We encountered another Barathes the Palmyrene back in Chapter 2 on a tombstone from Coria (Corbridge) and noted that many identify these two men as one and the same. You will notice that there is a rather marked difference in quality, style and cost between Barathes the *vexillarius'* funerary marker and this monument to Regina. If this is the same person, it raises many questions about why his own tombstone was so plain by comparison and contained none of the Palmyrene script he had taken care to have added to Regina's epitaph – perhaps Barathes had died rather unexpectedly, or perhaps by the time of his own death he was financially much less well off.

We next learn that Regina herself was not from Palmyra but had actually come from one of the Celtic tribes in the south-east of Britain: the Catuvellaunians. So, Regina is not quite as far from home as Barates, though she has evidently endured much over her thirty years. How did she end up enslaved in her own homeland? Allason-Jones thinks the likeliest explanation is that her parents had sold her into slavery at a young age, a practice that was technically illegal under Roman law until the early fourth century but was nonetheless widespread in the centuries beforehand.[7] She has then accompanied Barates at some point to the north of the province, and, having been freed and married, begun her next role as wife to a well-travelled and evidently rather wealthy Syrian within Roman society. The inscription records that she was 30 years old at the time of her death, though this is likely to be an estimate – 30 years old is the most commonly given age for women on tombstones from the Western Roman Empire.[8]

The Palmyrene script beneath the Latin repeats some of the same information but offers more of an emotional lament on the passing of his wife. It can be difficult to gauge genuine emotion over epigraphic convention – as we will see in some of the tombstones later in this chapter – but here Barates has found a way to both express and personalise his grief for his wife's passing. Why include it if few others would be able to read it? Well, for Barates, the question would more likely be, why not? It is an interesting example of the self-presentation of the dedicator being woven into the memorialisation of the deceased: Regina herself is neither Roman nor Palmyrene by birth,

Fig. 4.1 Tombstone of Regina, on display at the Arbeia Fort and Museum in South Shields.

though depending on the age at which she was enslaved, she may have only ever really known these languages. Her bilingual epitaph thus captures the complex merging of identities – and the ways in which they were represented – that came about from the wide movement, subjugation and interactions of people across the vast empire. This merging of cultural identities can also be clearly seen in the design of Regina's magnificent tombstone, from what she wears to the objects she holds.

Between two decorated columns, Regina sits on a high-backed wicker chair. She once gazed out at the viewer directly, though now only a blank remnant of her face remains. She is dressed in fine clothes and jewellery, all of which are carefully carved in much more detail than we often find on Romano-British tombstones. What is immediately clear from her outfit is that she is not dressed in the attire of a typical Roman lady. Regina wears a sleeved tunic, which falls over her knees down to the floor. Over the tunic, she also wears a calf-length cloak or coat, which has been pulled on over the head rather than draped around the shoulders. This is also sleeved. It has been identified as possibly a version of a Gallic coat – a thick outer garment worn in the northern provinces – which would certainly make sense for life on the chilly north-east coast.[9] The stonemason has taken great care with the drapery of the fabric; it is notable that Regina does not wear brooches to affix her clothing, a detail that aligns with a date towards the end of the second century, when this was going out of style.[10]

Regina's clothing is complemented by a selection of impressive – and noticeable – pieces of jewellery. On each wrist you can see that she is wearing a rather chunky bracelet that looks to be made from twisted metal – these are cable or torc-twisted bands, often made from copper alloy or even gold.[11] She also wears a torc around her neck. These large twisted-metal neck adornments are most commonly associated with the Celts and were worn by both men and women – indeed, a statue head recovered from the nearby fort of Condercum (Benwell) depicts the unique Romano-British deity Antenociticus, who is carved in a Celtic style and wears a torc around his neck. Regina herself, as a Catuvellaunian woman by birth, may have owned or even later commissioned this style of jewellery for herself as a way of reflecting her own ethnicity. Thus, although it has been noted that the torc had fallen out of fashion by this period and may simply be an anachronistic detail, there was also evidently some precedent for using it in art in the region as a way of signalling a hybrid Celtic-Roman cultural background.[12]

It is worth remembering here too that in the tombstone's original painted form, these accessories would have been even more visible. The jewellery worn by Regina would have acted as a clear indicator of her wealth and status at the time of her death – and by implication also reflecting her husband's wealth and status – contrasting sharply with her former status as slave. Her new status is also emphasised by the item that sits on the floor to her right: you can see on the tombstone that she reaches down with her right hand to open the lid of a box. This sturdy little wooden box has reinforced edging, a decorative crescent and a large lock on the front. This subtly tells the viewer that it was used to store items – like Regina's jewellery or other precious objects – that were valuable enough to need securing. The box shown beside Regina may well be her own personal jewellery box, which she is in the process of opening or closing – perhaps hinting that she has many more trinkets than those that are shown here on her person.[13]

While Regina may not be dressed in the style of a typical Roman woman, there are a handful of other objects on her tombstone that could perhaps show more of an alignment with Roman ideals when it came to the roles and responsibilities of the woman within the household. In her left hand she holds a distaff and spindle, the tools of wool spinning. On the floor to her left is a wicker basket filled with balls of wool. Instruments of spinning and weaving often appear on gravestones for, or in the grave depositions of, many ancient women all across the empire; many writers (mostly elite Roman men) draw a clear link between a virtuous woman and her wool-working skills. All of this reflects the idealised image of the industrious Roman *matrona* (a respectable wife): she was responsible for the domestic production of clothes for all members of her household.[14] This task more than any other came to symbolise the woman's devotion to – as well as effective management of – her household. Even beyond the domestic sphere, textile production remained a firmly gendered task in the Roman imagination. For Regina to hold these symbols of the ideal Roman wife emphasises her role within her marriage and her household. It also presents Regina how Barates – and even possibly Regina herself – wished for her to be seen and remembered: she may not have been a freeborn Roman, but she was nonetheless to be memorialised as a paragon of Roman virtue.

Any of these objects depicted on the tombstone may well have been buried with Regina, too. A small collection of personal objects recovered from one of the late fourth-century graves at the same cemetery showed signs of originally having been buried in a small wooden box. Nine bracelets, six finger rings, a string of beads, an iron chain, a knife and a purse had been deposited with the deceased; of the nine bracelets, two were cabled in style – one made from two copper alloy wires twisted together, the other from three of the same.[15] This grave also contained a jet distaff and spindle whorl, the tools of the virtuous Roman woman also wielded by Regina. No other Romano-British tombstone depicts a woman holding the same objects as Regina, but here we have the same objects interred with the deceased instead. This raises some intriguing questions about the performativity of the tombstone: is burying the objects with the deceased inside the grave more of a personal act than commissioning their representation on the funerary monument?

There is another region in which women are often depicted on the tombstone holding the same objects as Regina – indeed, even clutching the distaff and spindle in the same hand (left) with the same posing of the fingers: Palmyra.[16] Has Barates commissioned the monument based on his own – very distinct – vision of what his wife's tombstone should look like? Or is there another Palmyrene at Arbeia who also happened to be a stonemason? The design and script on the Regina's tombstone has led many to conclude the latter – particularly when considered alongside the elegant Palmyrene-influenced tombstone of Victor, which we saw in the previous chapter.

A CELTIC DAUGHTER

'VEDICA'

An impressive tombstone from Verbeia (Ilkley) offers another glimpse of life for a native Celtic woman in Roman Britain, this time from among the Cornovii people.[17] The stone was discovered towards the end of the nineteenth century by workmen creating ornamental gardens at the back of the Rose and Crown inn: it had been buried face-down about 0.5 metres below the surface of the soil as part of the foundations of a wall.[18] The towering sandstone monument measures over 1.5 metres tall, and like Regina's tombstone is mostly taken up by a large seated portrait of the deceased. There had been some damage to either side of the stone as well as to the inscription underneath the portrait – especially the second line, which records the name of the deceased.

Inscription
DIS MANIBVS
VED[.] IC[...] RICONIS FILIA
ANNORVM XXX C CORNOVIA
H S E

Expanded Text
Dis Manibus
Ved[.] ic[..] [..] riconis filia
annorum XXX civis Cornovia
hic situs est

Translation
TO THE SPIRITS OF THE DEAD
Ved[.] ic[...] daughter of [...] rico
30 years old
a citizen of the Cornovii
HERE SHE LIES

The inscription begins with the unabbreviated dedication to the spirits of the dead, here suggesting an earlier date in the first to early second centuries when this was the more popular epigraphic habit. The second line has suffered the most damage to the lettering, which makes her name difficult to recover: it has been variously reconstructed as Velvica or Velnica, but she has become informally known as 'Vedica'.

The rest of the line contains her filiation – she is identified as *filia* ('daughter'), presumably of the name that would have been written just before this. The beginning of this name is lost so we can only see the ending *–riconis*. This name would have been written in the genitive form to indicate possession – i.e. daughter *of* [name]. In Latin, a group of nouns known as the third declension have the genitive singular ending *-is*, so we know that the nominative form (i.e. the regular name) likely had a different ending. What this would have been, however, is tricky to narrow down. Many third declension forms have their own particular nominative ending – there is not one specific pattern that applies to all nouns in this group.[19] I have opted for restoring the name as ending with '[...] rico'.[20] But it may well be something else entirely, especially given that this is likely a Romanised spelling of a Celtic name.

'Vedica' was 30 years old at the time of her death. Sound familiar? We noted above with Regina's tombstone that this is the most common age given for women in the Roman west. It is likely a rounded estimate of her actual age. We are also told more about her background: she originally comes from a Celtic tribe called the Cornovii who were based in and around modern-day Shropshire with a capital at Viroconium Cornoviorum (Wroxeter). In his study of the Cornovii, Webster notes that Virico was a well-attested male personal name in Gallic sources. He hypothesises that the Latinised name of the tribe's capital may carry the inherent meaning of 'the town of Virico' in reference to an earlier ruler.[21] This opens up the possibility for restoring the name of the father on our tombstone to 'Virico' – with Vedica's family connection to a powerful Cornovian plausibly explaining why she was afforded such a grand tombstone. This is a tidy solution but possibly relies on a few too many assumptions. Perhaps the more pressing question is that if Vedica has come from a wealthy Cornovian family, what has brought her up north to Verbeia?

Crucially, she is not identified at any point on the tombstone as a wife: she is memorialised as a daughter. This makes it unlikely that she has moved north because of a marriage. Her father may have relocated with the army – indeed, the First Cohort of Cornovians (Cohors I Cornoviorum) was the only unit of native recruits known to have actually been stationed in the province. Records place it at Pons Aelius (Newcastle upon Tyne) on Hadrian's Wall by the fourth century, but they would certainly have been deployed elsewhere in the centuries beforehand.[22] Or her father may have been a successful trader who moved – possibly with the army – for work. The first timber fort at Verbeia was built around AD 80 and occupied for about twenty years before it was abandoned. It was reoccupied and rebuilt in stone from the latter half of the second century onwards. A civilian settlement (*vicus*) developed to the south of the fort; it is here Vedica would have lived.

The majority of the tombstone is occupied by Vedica's portrait. Like Regina, she is seated on a high-backed chair, facing the viewer directly. She wears a long-sleeved tunic, which reaches down to her ankles. Over this, she wears a thick cloak, which looks like it has been pulled on over the head rather than fastened around the shoulders. It falls down over her knees in a triangular cut, the point of the cloth almost reaching to her feet. She holds a small object in her left hand, which rests on her lap, though the detail of this is now lost. She wears a torc, the Celtic neck ring. The upper portion of her face and head survives, with her eyes carved in the Roman style. The nose and mouth have been damaged. Her hair is perhaps one of the most interesting features: wavy and thick, it has been brushed back from her face and gathered under an elaborate headdress. Two long plaits cascade down either side of her head and all the way down to her lap. She gently draws both plaits together in front of her chest with her raised right hand. Whether the plaits are her own hair or are adornments attached to the headdress is difficult to ascertain given the condition of the stone. Traditional depictions of Roman women often show elaborate hairstyles but usually plaited hair is swept up into a hairstyle; here, the length and style of the plaits (whether real or not) could reflect a more local fashion. The deliberate gesture of grasping the hair with the hand has been compared to Romano-British depictions of the goddess Venus, though the latter usually pulls her loose flowing locks towards her rather than such lengthy plaits.[23]

Vedica's tombstone is another remarkable example of the layered identities individuals could assume during the Roman occupation of Britannia. Her tombstone presents her in the manner of an elite Roman woman, letting the ancient viewer immediately know that she is from an important and successful family. Yet she does not lose her Celtic roots: this is made visually and textually clear in both her dress and her explicit identification as a Cornovian, with her own filiation, on the epitaph. Unlike Regina, she is not memorialised as an ideal wife, but rather as a daughter from a tribe that predated the arrival of the Romans. Her family may have adapted to certain Roman ways of life, but they have not lost their connection to their own past.

A STRIKING NAME

The layered cultural identities across the province were not only visible in grand funerary portraits. Many of the surviving monuments offer an insight into the merging of those from Celtic backgrounds with a new kind of Roman society even if they do not depict the deceased themselves. The epitaph on a recently discovered limestone monument from Corinium

Dobunnorum (Cirencester) dated to the second century AD records an especially striking name.

Inscription	Expanded Text
I	*I*
D M	*Dis Manibus*
BODICACIA	*Bodicacia*
CONIVNX	*coniunx*
VIXIT ANNO	*vixit anno-*
S XXVII	*s XXVII*

Translation

I

TO THE SPIRITS OF THE DEAD

Bodicacia

wife

she lived

27 years

The lettering of the epitaph is not especially well spaced and has some interesting peculiarities. The very top line, for example, contains only the slightly off-centre single letter I. Could the stonemason have started to carve the D in the very top line before changing his mind, leaving an errant line? Possibly, but a closer look at the letterforms shows the same flourished crossbars as the other I forms later in the inscription. Could it form part of the initial abbreviated dedication? The alternative D I M (*Dis Inferis Manibus* – 'to the spirits of the dead below') appears on tombstones across the empire, and indeed is found in Britannia on a tombstone from Carlisle.[24] Perhaps our stonemason has opted for the less common arrangement I D M (*inferis Dis Manibus*)? This form is otherwise unattested as an abbreviation on Romano-British tombstones but does appear elsewhere in the empire.[25] But even then, the irregular spacing makes it seem unlikely that the three letters were intended to be read as part of the same abbreviation, leaving the meaning of the single I a mystery.

On the next line down, the abbreviated D M sits to the left side of the panel rather than in the centre, leaving a large gap across the rest of the line.

By contrast, the fifth line is overfilled, pushing the final *s* of the word *annos* just over into the next line. The shaping of the N is especially noticeable throughout the inscription for its markedly more cursive style. On the stone itself, the guidelines cut into the surface for the lettering are still visible, suggesting the work of a less experienced stonecutter.

The inscription is brief and lacking in much detail. We have the dedication to the spirits of the dead, followed by the name of the deceased: Bodicacia. This striking name would undoubtedly have been Celtic in origin (though is not to be confused with the more famous Boudicca!). Skeletal remains were discovered beneath the stone, but after analysis were revealed to belong to a man from the fourth century AD. The stone had likely been moved from its original location to be reused later as a grave marker.[26]

The tombstone itself has nonetheless survived in good condition. Measuring just over 1.3 metres tall, the majority of the stone is taken up by the inscription, set within a recessed rectangular panel. This is topped with a crested gable, which contains the carved head of the Roman god Oceanus. The head has been defaced at some point though the god's long flowing locks and crab-claw horns remain clear. As a mythological figure, Oceanus was a primordial Titan god of fresh waters: he gave his name to the great deep-flowing river Oceanus, which encircled the entire world. The entrance to the underworld, to which all souls journeyed, lay far across the river Oceanus. His appearance within this tombstone's pediment could thus be a nod to this mythological journey – merging once again native Celtic peoples with highly Roman funerary customs and beliefs. Indeed, as we will see in the next tombstone, imagery of the sea was one of the many iconographical choices for monuments to the dead.

A DINNER PARTY

A fantastic tombstone from Deva Victrix (Chester) captures a lively scene of eternal celebration for a woman called Curatia Dionysia.[27] Like many of the monuments from Deva, it was discovered rebuilt in the western section of the city's north wall. Despite having been recycled as building material, the tombstone survived in one full piece with its details fairly well preserved:

standing over 1 metre tall, it features a large full-body portrait of the deceased within an arched recess. This scene occupies more than half of the stone; beneath it, a neatly carved inscription is set within a rectangular panel.

<table>
<tr><td align="center">Inscription</td><td align="center">Expanded Text</td></tr>
<tr><td align="center">D M</td><td align="center">Dis Manibus</td></tr>
<tr><td align="center">CVRATIA DINY</td><td align="center">Curatia Diny-</td></tr>
<tr><td align="center">SIA VIX AN XXXX</td><td align="center">sia vixit annos XXXX</td></tr>
<tr><td align="center">H F C</td><td align="center">heres faciendum curavit</td></tr>
</table>

Translation
TO THE SPIRITS OF THE DEAD
Curatia Dionysia
lived 40 years
her heir took care to set this up

The lettering is confident and clear, and some letters – like the Y – show a particular flourish. Decorative leaves surround the abbreviations on the first and last line, while triangular interpuncts separate the words on the second and third lines. The text is centred and well spaced. All words except the name of the deceased are abbreviated.

The tombstone is dedicated to a woman called Curatia Dinysia. It seems likely that the second name is Dionysia, a well-attested feminine version of the Greek name Dionysus, which has been slightly misspelled – possibly reflecting the manner of pronunciation. We are told that she lived for forty years – another rounded number – and that her heir has set up this monument for her. We are given no other information about her life in the inscription, but we do have a lively accompanying representation of the deceased. This motif on funerary sculpture is often referred to by scholars as *totenmahl* ('death feast'). Popular in early Greek art of the Archaic and Classical periods, the motif was very much a provincial phenomenon during the Roman imperial period and was closely linked with military communities.[28] Almost thirty examples have been recovered from Roman Britain in varying conditions, the highest concentration (twelve) coming from Deva Victrix specifically.

Here, Curatia Dionysia appears in the centre of the scene, reclining on a high-backed couch in the middle of a dinner party. She rests on her left side, propped up by her left elbow, which leans on a cushion. Her face has been destroyed but would have once looked out directly at the viewer as she raises a cup with her right hand. Curatia is dressed comfortably and in the similar provincial style of Regina and Vedica: her sleeved ankle-length tunic falls in loose folds around her legs and arms. Her hair is neatly swept back over her ears and gathered behind her head. A three-legged table is positioned in front of the couch for her to rest her drink on, while the recessed space in which she sits is very much decorated for a celebration: two festoons of gathered leaves hang behind her, and perched on these swooping garlands are two doves. Two figures called Tritons also appear above her: these were sea gods who had the upper body of a human and the lower tail of a fish. Each Triton slithers down the curve of the arch with its huge serpentine tail; their bodies are turned back so that they face each other as they either blow into or drink out of conches.[29] Tritons often appear in mythological stories, playfully accompanying other sea creatures and deities through the waters,

playing music, or sometimes even drunk and dancing. Their imagery on the tombstone could draw upon all of these features: the rejoicing and fun-loving Tritons may well be accompanying our party-loving Curatia as she embarks on her own journey across the seas to the underworld.

The little extra details added around Curatia's *totenmahl* scene here capture a range of sounds and movements, creating a joyful and lively image of her funerary banquet. Just as the dining scene of Aurelius Lucius in Chapter 1 personalised his environment with objects that were important to his presentation as a soldier – his weapons – the décor around

Fig. 4.2 Tombstone of Curatia Dionysia, on display at the Grosvenor Museum, Chester.

Curatia may perhaps offer us a glimpse of her own life. Interestingly, a number of *totenmahl* tombstones survive from Deva specifically: these all depict the same basic composition of the deceased enjoying an eternal dinner party, leading to suggestions that there was a workshop in the ancient city that specialised in this particular scene. Many of these were created for women and shared similar decorative imagery beyond the basic elements of the motif. The tombstone of Fesonia Severiana, for example, depicts the deceased reclining on a high-backed couch in the same pose as Curatia: she leans on her left, propped up on her left elbow, and raises a cup in her right hand.[30] The face is not destroyed this time but is badly worn; despite this, Fesonia Severiana still gazes out towards the viewer. Her hair is brushed back away from her face and she also wears a sleeved long tunic. Above her, a dove perches on a hanging garland – there may have been a matching second dove, but the top left corner of the recess has been lost. In a variation to the scene's composition, another woman is shown standing behind the couch: her position here along with her smaller stature suggests she is one of the deceased's slaves, attending to her mistress's needs during the party.

Another example from Deva shows the deceased once more reclining in the midst of a dinner party, leaning on her left side as she raises a cup with her right hand. This tombstone no longer has an inscription, so we have no information about the name or age of the deceased. But like the others, she is dressed in a long and loose-sleeved tunic, and her hair is gathered neatly around her head. Her face is not deliberately damaged but badly worn, though the shape of her rounded eyes can still be seen looking directly out at the viewer. She rests on another high-backed couch with a three-legged table positioned to the front. In a further variation to the standard scene, a

Fig. 4.3 Tombstone of the seashell woman, on display at the Grosvenor Museum, Chester.

huge scallop shell hangs behind her, interestingly positioned between her and the couch back.

We also find the same composition and additional features – including the oversized shell – appearing on a tombstone dedicated to two young sisters from Deva, Restita and Martia; we will see more about their monument in Chapter 5. The fortunate survival of this group of tombstones provides an insight into the funerary scenes that became popular for representing the deceased – especially women – in Roman Chester. The inherent meaning of the dining scene is often debated: does it represent the deceased as they had enjoyed life? Or is it more of an aspirational depiction? Should it be understood as the funerary banquet? Or does it show how the deceased is spending their time now they are unfettered from their daily life? It is impossible to know definitively, but this does not make the motif any less impactful. Imagining it from the viewer's perspective, it must have been a remarkable sight to come across while passing by the cemetery: whatever the individual meaning of each stone, the mood shared across every interpretation is one of celebration and enjoyment.

The popularity of sea imagery across many of these scenes adds another layer of symbolism to decipher, too. Deva was close to the sea and the legionary fortress occupied a strategic position by the river Dee, so it would not be surprising for local artisans to draw upon the surrounding natural environment for their inspiration. However, we also find this imagery appearing on tombstones of this type from elsewhere in the province. Over in Eboracum (York), the upper remaining fragment of an elegant banqueting scene shows a wife and her husband reclining together on the same couch – within an arched recess that is surmounted by dolphins.[31]

As we saw with Curatia's tombstone, different sea creatures – like the Tritons – had their own qualities and characteristics from their many mythological stories, and were often linked with specific deities. Dolphins were renowned as compassionate and helpful creatures of the sea in many ancient tales; they are also linked with a number of gods and goddesses, including Neptune, Apollo, Bacchus and Venus. Shells and sea creatures on tombstones are often more broadly interpreted as evoking the long journey the dead must make across the vast ocean in order to reach the underworld. But considering the intertwining of imagery across these tombstones for different women in the province, it could also be the case that the additional decorative details – like the shells or indeed the doves – were intended to evoke the goddess Venus.

Venus – the Roman counterpart of Aphrodite – was born from the sea foam after the castrated genitals of Ouranos fell from the sky into the waves below. She regularly appears alongside sea creatures or water deities; in one particularly impressive fresco from first-century AD Pompeii, the goddess reclines inside a giant shell as it floats on the sea's waves.[32] In many depictions, she is also often accompanied by the dove, her sacred bird. Venus certainly had a presence in Romano-British art, too: a variety of mosaics, reliefs, statuettes and jewellery featuring the goddess have been found all across the province. In the Rudston Venus mosaic, the goddess is accompanied by a Triton, as well as a variety of animals and four doves. In the Kingscote Venus mosaic, she is encircled by rolling waves, while dolphins and other sea creatures swim nearby. And on the Hemsworth Venus mosaic, Venus emerges from a large scallop shell, a long blue cloak billowing behind her in the sea wind. She is surrounded by a decorative arch of rolling waves, while dolphins and fish swim overhead. A striking relief from Bremenium fort on Hadrian's Wall shows the goddess bathing and washing her hair with two nymph attendants, while a now lost relief from Caerleon depicted the goddess seated and holding a dolphin in her right hand. Over 400 pipe-clay figurines of Venus have also been discovered at many sites in Britannia, some even deposited at grave sites.

Venus was the goddess of love, fertility and beauty, but she also held a particular civic significance to the Romans, which set her apart from her Greek counterpart Aphrodite. As the mother of the mythological hero Aeneas, Venus was invoked by emperors such as Augustus as a way of legitimising their position through claimed divine descent. In this way, she came to represent not just Roman imperial power but also motherhood, and over time acquired a more 'matronly' character as a figure of modesty and virtue – qualities that as we shall shortly see were very much prized by the Romans in their representations of the ideal wife.[33] By adding the iconography of the goddess into this stock *totenmahl* 'death dinner' scene, these tombstones thus add a further layer of information about the presentation of women – idealised or real – and the qualities that were associated with them both in life and in death. As we will see in the inscriptions that follow, some tombstones chose to make this much more explicit through their choice of language.

A FAMILY PORTRAIT

A busy scene of family life occupies more than half of this tombstone from Eboracum, in honour of a woman called Julia Velva.[34] It was uncovered during work to create a new road in 1922 and remains even now an impressive sepulchral monument. Standing at over 1.5 metres tall by just under 1 metre wide, it features a snapshot of not just the deceased but their whole family in a variation of the dinner party scene, all set within a canopied niche. The inscription has been added within a recessed rectangular panel underneath the scene.

Inscription	Expanded Text
D M	*Dis Manibus*
IVLIE VELVE PIENTISSI	*Julie Velve pientissi-*
ME VIXIT AN L AVREL	*me vixit annos L Aurelius*
MERCVRIALIS HER FACI	*Mercurialis heres faci-*
VNDVM CVRAVIT VIVVS	*undum curavit vivus*
SIBI ET SVIS FECIT	*sibi et suis fecit*

Translation
TO THE SPIRITS OF THE DEAD
For Julia Velva
she lived most dutifully
50 years old
Aurelius Mercurialis, her heir,
took care to set this up
for himself and his family
while he was still alive

Following the abbreviated dedication to the spirits of the dead, we find the name of the deceased: Julia Velva. This is an interesting name combining the typically Roman with the more provincial as the Vel- root is often identified as Celtic in origin (as with the partially recorded name 'Vel—' we

Fig. 4.4 Tombstone of Julia Velva, on display at the Yorkshire Museum in York.

saw on an earlier tombstone). Julia Velva is described having lived her fifty years most dutifully – the superlative *pientissime* lets us as the viewer know that she adhered to a core Roman virtue of duty throughout her relatively long life. This is all we are told about Julia herself on the inscription: there is no identification of her by role such as wife, daughter or mother. The remaining lines of the inscription instead focus on the man who has set up this grand monument. He is identified as Aurelius Mercurialis, the heir to Julia Velva. He records on the epitaph that he set up the tombstone expressly for himself and his family while he was still living, making it clear that he is a close relation of Julia. Another son-in-law, or nephew, perhaps? The lack of clear relationship between the deceased and the dedicator, as well as the use of the phrase 'lived most dutifully', has been interpreted by some as an indication that Julia may even have been the freedwoman of Mercurialis.[35]

On the relief that accompanies the inscription, Julia Velva appears towards the back of the rather busy scene. At first glance, it looks as though she is standing behind the couch, but she is actually reclining on it: she leans on her left side, propping up her head with her left arm. The couch is relatively plain but has a thick mattress and cushions. Julia's face is only lightly worn. She has large, rounded eyes and neatly carved features; her hair is parted in the centre and voluminously brushed back behind her head. The details of her garments are difficult to discern in the rough gritstone, but she holds a cup in her right hand.

In front of the couch is the usual three-legged table, depicted upright rather than at a skewed angle, laden with dishes of food. Another larger table with clawed feet sits at the head of the couch, in front of which stands a male bearded figure – presumably Aurelius Mercurialis himself. He is dressed in a knee-length tunic and wears a cloak wrapped around his shoulders, a length of which hangs down to the front. On his feet are soft boots and he holds a scroll in his right hand, perhaps intended to indicate his status as the heir. Next to Mercurialis stands a much smaller figure who holds a wine jug in their left hand: this is likely a slave, attending to their mistress as she enjoys her banquet. To the left of the scene is another figure, this time a woman seated in a high-backed wicker chair. She has an elegant hairstyle and wears a long-sleeved tunic, which reaches down to her feet. In her hands she holds a small bird. Was this perhaps the wife of Mercurialis? We have already seen examples of tombstones that feature seated wives on similar wicker chairs; she may well have been the family to which Mercurialis was referring when he described setting up the monument during his own lifetime.

A FAITHFUL WIFE

During excavations for the North Eastern Railway at York in the late nineteenth century, workers discovered the fully intact gritstone coffin of a Roman woman called Julia Fortunata.[36] The large rectangular sarcophagus was over 2 metres in length and was still covered by its original gabled lid. As both the receptacle for the deceased as well as their funerary monument, the coffin would have once formed part of a tomb in a wealthy area of the cemetery that overlooked the river Ouse. An inscription set within a recessed panel recorded the name and role of the deceased on one of the coffin's long sides. Skeletal remains were present inside the coffin but after examination turned out to belong to a man, indicating that the coffin had later been reused.

Inscription
IVL FORTUNATE DOMO
SARDINIA VEREC DIO
GENI FIDA CONIVNCTA
MARITO

Expanded Text
Julia Fortunate domo
Sardinia Verecundio Dio-
geni fida coniuncta
marito

Translation
For Julia Fortunata
her home was Sardinia
a faithful wife to
Verecundius Diogenes
her husband

The lettering is confidently carved and shows some flourish in the forms; small triangular interpuncts separate words on the first and second lines. The inscription sits centrally in a recessed panel between two decorative pelta motifs. The inscription offers us a small glimpse into Julia Fortunata's background as we are told that she has originally come from Sardinia. This large Mediterranean island had been seized by the Romans in 238 BC and then incorporated into a province along with Corsica in 227 BC. Despite revolts, the Romans kept control of the island. In the early imperial period, Sardinia was separated off from Corsica to become its own province.

Almost as much space is given to identifying Julia Fortunata's husband, Verecundius Diogenes. He would have been the person responsible for commissioning the sarcophagus. He is also presumably the source of our description of Julia herself as a faithful wife to her husband. The final three words given here (*fida coniuncta marito*) carry a dactylic rhythm and have been compared to the end of a hexameter line from the Roman poet Catullus. Through this short descriptor, Julia is memorialised as having fulfilled her role as a wife. The deliberate choice to end the inscription with these melodic words – rather than an abbreviation or stock phrase – reflect some level of individuality while also perhaps nodding to the husband's literary interests. *Fida*, the adjective that describes Julia Fortunata here, represents one of the most important Roman values: *fides*. This is much more than just 'faithfulness' for the Romans: it incorporated loyalty, trustworthiness, sincerity and honesty as the basis for successful social relationships.[37] Within a marriage, this was essential – not just in terms of marital fidelity (though this, of course, was exceptionally important) but also in how much a husband could trust his wife to properly manage the household in his absence.

Interestingly in this case, we do also have records of Verecundius Diogenes' coffin. It had actually been discovered in York in the sixteenth century, but was then lost before the end of the eighteenth century. Records from the time fortunately preserve the inscription as well as a sketch; through this, we find out a bit more about why Verecundius and his wife were afforded such grand tombs.

Inscription

M VEREC DIOGENES SEVIR COL
EBOR IDEMQ MOR T CIVES BITVRIX
CVBVS HAEC SIBI VIVVS FECIT

Expanded Text

Marcus Verecundius Diogenes sevir coloniae Eboracensis idemque Morinorum et cives Biturix Cubus haec sibi vivus fecit

Translation

Marcus Verecundius Diogenes, *sevir* of Colonia Eboracum and likewise Colonia Morinorum citizen of the Bituriges Cubi he made these during his own lifetime

Verecundius' inscription records that he had been a *sevir* of Eboracum and Tarvenna (referred to here as *colonia Morinorum*). The *sevir* was one of six men who served on a board for municipal, colonial or military matters; Verecundius thus seems to have held the status of a 'minor dignitary' in two cities.[38] This explains the impressive stone sarcophagi that he has commissioned for both himself and his wife during his own lifetime – and which he refers to when he uses the plural 'these' (*haec*) on his own inscription. Verecundius is not from Sardinia like his wife; instead, he identifies himself as a citizen of the Bituriges Cubi, a powerful tribe from Gaul who were incorporated into the Roman province Gallia Aquitania. Many *seviri* – especially those associated with the imperial cult – were wealthy freedmen. This may be the case here, too, given the mixture of Roman (Marcus), Gallic (Verecundius) and Greek (Diogenes) in his written name.

Verecundius has taken care to ensure both his and his wife's origins are recorded on the epitaphs, offering us another insight into the movement of people across the empire that enabled a man – possibly even a freedman – from Gaul and a woman from Sardinia to settle in Britannia. Even with these layers of cultural identity, we see that Julia Fortunata is nonetheless prominently memorialised as the virtuous Roman wife: faithful and trustworthy, she proved such a stalwart companion to her successful husband that he built his own sarcophagus beside hers while he was still living.

A DEARLY BELOVED WIFE

Another Roman woman who made her reappearance in the nineteenth century is Aurelia Aureliana. Her buff sandstone monument was found during work on the 'great mail-road' between Penrith and Carlisle in 1829; it lay more than 1 metre beneath the soil on Gallows Hill – once the site of the cemetery of Luguvalium (Carlisle) – and had been buried face-down.[39] Although it showed signs of extensive burning to the back, the tombstone and its details had nonetheless survived in very good condition. It measures over 1.5 metres tall and features a full-body portrait of the deceased standing within an arched recess. The arch is supported by a column on each side, while on top of each column sits a large pinecone. Beneath the portrait is the inscription, which is set within a rectangular recessed panel.

Inscription
D M AVR AVRELIA VIXSIT
ANNOS XXXXI VLPIVS
APOLINARIS CONIVGI CARISSIME
POSVIT

Expanded Text
Dis Manibus Aurelia Aureliana vixsit
annos XXXXI Ulpius
Apolinaris coniugi carissime
posuit

Translation
TO THE SPIRITS OF THE DEAD
Aurelia Aureliana
lived 41 years

Ulpius Apolinaris
set this up for his dearly beloved wife

We have the abbreviated dedication to the spirits of the dead, followed on the same line by the name of the deceased: Aurelia Aureliana. We are told that she lived for forty-one years. The verb written here for 'lived' (*vixsit*) is a variation on the usual spelling that appears on inscriptions across the empire. Aurelia's monument has been set up by her husband, a man named as Ulpius Apolinaris. He adds the affectionate and unabbreviated remark *coniugi carissima* to describe Aurelia, his dearly beloved wife. We are told nothing else in the inscription about her life beyond this.

Just as we have a collection of acceptable phrases to draw upon when expressing bereavement and grief in the modern world, so too did the Romans. This is especially clear to see on tombstones for women: many inscriptions draw upon the same phrases to express their loss while also recording variations of these fixed socio-cultural virtues to which all women were expected to aspire. One of these set phrases is *coniugi carissima* – 'a dearly beloved wife'. Does it show genuine affection? Or is it simply a matter of convention? There is no reason to suppose it cannot have been both: the bereaved husband was tasked with the job of memorialising his spouse and may have had many options to choose from in terms of phrasing. Why this phrase over any other? It may not frame the wife's marital

Fig. 4.5 Tombstone of Aurelia Aureliana, on display at the Great North Museum: Hancock in Newcastle upon Tyne.

virtues as prominently as some of the other choices – like *fida* – but it does emphasise the exemplary relationship between the two as well as the honour and duty of the living husband to his deceased wife.

The portrait of Aurelia offers us a glimpse into life up along the northern frontier for the many women who called it their home. She stands facing the viewer directly. Her face is worn but still retains its features, which show a more Celtic style of artistic representation – the eyes in particular appear large and rounded. Her hair is gathered back off her face and hangs neatly down behind her ears, resting just above her shoulders. Aurelia is dressed in warm clothing: her plain but voluminous cloak – the Gallic coat again – is sleeved and unbelted. It reaches down to her ankles. On her feet are soft plain shoes. Aurelia pulls the fringed edge of her cloak across her chest with her right hand; in her left hand she holds a small but neatly carved bunch of poppies. In Greek and Roman mythology, poppies were linked with the god of sleep, Hypnos, and his twin brother Thanatos, the god of death. The Romans often portrayed Ceres, the goddess of agriculture and fertility, with poppies as well as wheat in both art and literature – for example, the poet Virgil mentions 'the poppy of Ceres' in his pastoral work *Georgics*.[40] Ceres was closely associated with the female virtues owing to her divine duties as well as her role as devoted mother to the goddess Proserpina – making her symbols an especially suitable choice for the memorial of a beloved wife (and perhaps also mother).

A SPOTLESS WIFE

For the next tombstone we head east from Luguvalium out along Hadrian's Wall to the fort of Magnis (Carvoran), where another exemplary wife called Aurelia had lived and died.[41] Her tombstone was unearthed in 1825 during work to the medieval tower house at Blenkinsopp Castle. It is a large rectangular monument that stands just over 1.5 metres tall; there is no portrait this time but there is a prominent epitaph spaced over nine lines that offers us more information about Aurelia's life.

Inscription	**Expanded Text**
D M	*Dis Manibus*
AVR T F AIAE	*Aureliae Titi filia Aiae*
D SALONAS	*domo Salonas*
AVR MARCVS	*Aurelis Marcus*
> OBSEQ CON	*centuria Obsequentis con-*
IVGI SANCTIS	*iugi sanctis-*
SIMAE QVAE VI	*simae quae vi-*
XIT ANNIS XXXIII	*xit annis XXXIII*
SINE VLLA MACVLA	*sine ulla macula*

Translation

TO THE SPIRITS OF THE DEAD
For Aurelia Aia daughter of Titus
her home was Salona
Aurelius Marcus
from Obsequens' century
(set this up) to his most pure wife
she lived 33 years
without any blemish

The lettering is mostly centred, if a little haphazard in execution: there are several lines where the stonecutter has run out of space and had to squash a tiny letterform in towards the end (5–8). The final line is also rather messier in form and may have been added by a different hand. The abbreviated dedication to the spirits of the dead is followed immediately by the name of the deceased, Aurelia Aia. Interestingly, Aurelia is also given a filiation as part of her name: she is identified as daughter of Titus (T F = *Titi filia*). We are also told that Aurelia originally comes from Salona. Salona (Colonia Martia Iulia Salona) was the capital of the Roman province of Dalmatia. This was a large territory that covered much of modern-day Croatia, Bosnia and Herzegovina, Montenegro and Serbia, as well as the northern region of Albania. Aurelia lived for thirty-three years: a specific number this time, though the numerals III have been added in a much smaller size to fit into the line.

Aurelia's tombstone has been erected by her husband, Aurelius Marcus. Given the pattern of naming, some have suggested that Aurelia is a freedwoman who had previously been enslaved to Aurelius.[42] He is a soldier in the army and describes himself as belonging to the century of a man called Obsequens. If Aurelius and Aurelia were indeed married, then this would point to a date from the third century AD onwards, after the marriage ban was lifted by the emperor Septimius Severus and all soldiers could legally marry – but of course, as we have seen on other tombstones, the use of the term husband or wife is not definite proof of legal union.[43] Aurelius does not identify his military unit by name. Several different units are attested at Magnis from inscriptions, including other tombstones from the civilian settlement (*vicus*) which developed beside the fort. Given Aurelia's origins, it is certainly tempting to link her husband with the Second Cohort of Dalmatians, which garrisoned the fort in the third century AD.[44] But as we saw with the tombstones of Julia Fortunata and her husband, there was no guarantee that both spouses came from the same place.

Aurelia is described as a 'most pure' wife (*coniugi sanctissimae*), the dedicator here choosing to use the superlative form of the adjective (*sancta*) to firmly emphasise her exemplary character. *Sancta* as a descriptor encompasses a range of interconnected qualities such as purity and holiness, and above all indicates someone of a morally good character. The final line reinforces this presentation of Aurelia by telling us that she also lived 'without any blemish' (*sine ulla macula*). This little phrase has been highlighted as possibly indicating evidence of Christian beliefs, especially when considered alongside the links to Salona, where there was an early tradition of Christianity.[45] But it is worth highlighting that the phrasing also appears in non-Christian literature: the Roman writer Cicero uses it in reference to (men's) character specifically.[46] While no other tombstone in the province has survived with this description for the deceased, we do find the same phrase as well as the shorter *sine macula* ('without blemish') used elsewhere in the empire by husbands on epitaphs for their wives.[47] Whatever the motivation – or religion – behind the phrasing on this tombstone, Aurelia Aia is eternally remembered as a wife of purest virtue and cleanest character.

A WELL-DESERVING WIFE (OR TWO?)

On a limestone monument from Lindum Colonia (Lincoln), we come face to face with not one but two Roman women.[48] The tombstone was discovered during building work in 1859: it had been recycled in the foundations of a wall in the lower Roman town. Although damaged, it is still a striking monument: measuring just over 1.3 metres in height, it features classical portrait busts of two women set within a gabled recess. Beneath them, a rectangular panel records two inscriptions, which look to have been cut at different times by different hands.

Inscription	Expanded Text
D M	*Dis Manibus*
VOLVSIA	*Volusia*
FAVSTINA	*Faustina*
C LIND V	*civis Lindensis vixit*
ANN XXVI	*annos XXVI*
M I D XXVI	*mensem I dies XXVI*
AVR SENE	*Aurelius Senecio*
CIO DEC OB	*decurio ob*
MERITA C P	*merita coniugi posuit*
D M	*Dis Manibus*
CL CATIOTVI	*Claudia Catiotui*
VIXTT A[.]	*vixit an-*
N LX[..]	*nnos LX[..]*

Translation
TO THE SPIRITS OF THE DEAD
Volusia Faustina
a citizen of Lindum
she lived 26 years, 1 month, 26 days
Aurelius Senecio, councillor,
set this up for his well-deserving wife
TO THE SPIRITS OF THE DEAD
Claudia (daughter of) Catiotuus
she lived 60 years

The first woman commemorated is Volusia Faustina. Her epitaph sits beneath the left portrait bust, which is slightly larger than the other and occupies the front position. We are told that she herself is a local woman who was born right there in Lindum. Lindum had originally been founded as a legionary fortress early in the Roman occupation, but before the end of the first century AD had become a *colonia* – a settlement for legionary veterans. Tomlin notes that her 'good Roman name' and her local background suggest she was descended from an army veteran.[49] We do not get a rounded number recording Volusia's age at the time of death, indeed quite the opposite: her age is carefully recorded as 26 years, 1 month, and 26 days. The tombstone has been erected by her husband, a man called Aurelius Senecio. He identifies himself as a decurion (*decurio*) but does not add details of any military unit, indicating that he is a civil decurion – an administrative role similar to our modern councillor – in the *colonia* at Lindum.

Volusia Faustina is commemorated for her role as wife. This time, she is praised as 'well-deserving' (*merita*). This term and its variations – especially *bene merens* – often appear on epitaphs for wives, daughters or mothers, and emphasises the way in which the deceased dutifully fulfilled the expectations of their role.[50] Here, the praise for her as a wife is further enhanced by the portrait that sits directly above her inscription. Volusia is dressed in a lighter and more traditionally Roman style than many of the women we have encountered so far. The carefully shaped direction of drapery on the bust shows that she is wearing a tunic, which is possibly covered with a *stola*. The *stola* was the attire of the respectable *matrona* (married woman) in Rome and as such, it became a visual marker of her conjugal faithfulness and modesty. It was a loose flowing garment without sleeves, which fastened at the shoulders and reached down to the feet. The *stola* was often worn with the *palla*, a long rectangular shawl that could be worn draped around the chest, shoulders, waist or head. Here, Volusia wears the *palla* over her left shoulder.

She also wears a large, beaded necklace. The strands of her wavy hair are neatly brushed back away from her face and gathered behind her head into a loose bun, the rolled edges of which are visible behind the ears just resting to the nape of the neck. Women usually kept their hair long and would wear it pinned up, though the style in which they did this varied greatly over time. Many followed the style of the imperial women, and naturally, each new empress needed to be differentiated on sculpture and coins through her own personal style. Volusia, despite living on the edges of the empire, has kept up to date with the latest trends; the wavy and low-rolled styling on her hair suggests the monument was erected in the mid-third century AD. The face has been damaged so that little detail remains beyond the oval lines of the eyes. The difference in the carving style to the head and the rest of the body suggests that it was perhaps a prefabricated tombstone that allowed personalised heads to be added to ready-made busts.[51] When viewed alongside her epitaph, Volusia's portrait certainly aligns with her description as the exemplary and well-deserving Roman wife. Yet she

Fig. 4.6 Tombstone of Volusia Faustina and Claudia, on display at the British Museum.

is not the only woman on the monument – so, who is the second woman?

She is identified on the second epitaph beneath the right portrait bust as Claudia, daughter of Catiotuus. This is obviously a different naming pattern than the first epitaph: could the single name and filiation perhaps suggest we have a woman of a different social class? Catiotuus has been described as an 'indigenous' name, which indicates she had likely been born in Britannia to a non-Roman family.[52] The only other information we have about Claudia is that she lived to at least 60 years old – damage to the inscription panel means we cannot see if there were any further numerals beyond LX. It is notable that with her older age she is nonetheless identified – and thus memorialised – on the inscription by her role as someone's daughter.

The lettering of Claudia's inscription is not as uniform or well spaced as that on Volusia's side, and has evidently been rather squashed in at some point afterwards. In her portrait she is dressed in the same clothing as Volusia, though she does not wear a necklace. Her hairstyle is different: it has been brushed into a centre parting and falls in the 'Julia Domna' style of ridged waves to either side of the head, which cover the ears. Although Claudia's face has also been damaged, the lines of her more rounded and enlarged eyes can still be seen – another feature that appeared on Julia Domna's portraiture. This is an interesting style when considered beside Volusia Faustina as it actually predates her hairstyle: Julia Domna was Roman empress in AD 193–211. However, if we consider that the tombstone may have been erected in the mid-third century, then Claudia's age at the time of her death would mean she had been a young woman during Julia Domna's reign, when she may have been influenced by her iconic hairstyle.

We are not given any explanation as to the relationship between the two women. Some have suggested they are mother and daughter: perhaps Volusia's father had married a local woman in Britannia when he settled in the *colonia* at Lindum. The identification of Claudia as a daughter rather than as Volusia's mother on the epitaph seems unusual; if that is the case, it could be a way for her to assert her own non-Roman lineage. Or perhaps Senecio as the presumed dedicator was simply less inclined to add an elaborate epitaph for his mother-in-law. If not a mother, though, then perhaps Claudia was a beloved – and unmarried – aunt? Others have wondered if Claudia was the second wife of Senecio, who would likely have remarried after the death of his young first wife. Her brief epitaph would certainly contrast sharply with Volusia's encomium as a well-deserving wife, if so. And some have viewed Claudia – given her manner of identification and her age, as well as her positioning behind Volusia and noticeable lack of jewellery – as a beloved slave or freedwoman who was honoured after her death by being buried with her mistress.

A MOST DEVOTED MOTHER

A rectangular sandstone panel, which had once been built into the fort wall at Habitancum (Risingham), commemorates the passing of a woman called Aurelia Lupula. It is a simple monument measuring just over 0.5 metres wide by 0.75 metres tall and it features an inscription within a recessed panel. There are seven lines of squarely cut text, underneath which four letters have been set within a small circle. An ivy leaf interpunct appears between the given names on the second line; the centre point holes are also visible in the letter O on the fifth and sixth lines.

Inscription
D M S
AVR LVPV
LE MATRI
PIISSIME
DIONYSIVS
FORTVNA
TVS FILIVS

S T
T L

Expanded Text
Dis Manibus sacrum
Aureliae Lupu-
lae matri
piissimae
Dionysius
Fortuna-
tus filius

sit tibi
terra levis

Translation
SACRED TO THE SPIRITS OF THE DEAD
For Aurelia Lupula
a most devoted mother
Dionysius Fortunatus
her son (set this up)
MAY THE EARTH LIE
LIGHT UPON YOU

Following the abbreviated dedication to the spirits of the dead, the name of the deceased is recorded: Aurelia Lupula. This time we do not have a wife but a mother, though you will notice Aurelia is described in similarly effusive terms as a most devoted (*piissimae*) mother using the superlative form of the adjective. We are not given any information about Aurelia's background, nor do we have an age recorded for her at the time of her death. Indeed, there is little else we are told about Aurelia except that the tombstone has been erected by her son, a man called Dionysius Fortunatus. He offers no information about himself other than his name. The two may have lived in the small civilian settlement (*vicus*) that developed beside the fort; several civilian tombstones – including some dedicated to children – have been found at the site, many also having been rebuilt into the fort walls. Another Aurelia Lupula is recorded on an inscription from Slovenia as the dedicator of a tombstone to her husband, Aurelius Victor, a 30-year-old legionary soldier who had died in battle. Could this be the same woman? Perhaps Aurelia had remarried a soldier who was then sent to Habitancum. We know that

Aurelia was a common name already, but Lupula less so: it appears forty-nine times on inscriptions across the empire, the majority coming from Africa and Gaul.[53] As a name, it is formed by the addition of the ending *-ula* onto an existing name, a common practice that could often signal affection as the suffix added a diminutive meaning ('little'). *Lupula* carries the meaning of 'little wolf', though in some usage it retained negative connotations as a term for a hag or witch (these meanings seem rather unlikely on a tombstone for a mother from her son!).

The detail added beneath the main inscription comprises four letters (S T T L) enclosed within a circle. This abbreviation stands for the phrase *sit tibi terra levis*, 'may the earth lie light upon you'. This had appeared in literature, developing into a popular abbreviation on funerary monuments across the empire from the first century AD onwards.

A LONG LIFE

A fragmentary stone from Lindum records the oldest known woman from Roman Britain.[54] It was discovered in 1830 after having been rebuilt into the Roman city walls; the upper section of the limestone has been lost but fortunately, the majority of the inscription remains.

Inscription	Expanded Text
D M	*Dis Manibus*
CLAVDIAE	*Claudiae*
CRYSIDI	*Crysidi*
VIXIT	*vixit*
AN LXXXX	*annos LXXXX*
HEREDES	*heredes*
P C	*ponendum curaverunt*

Translation
TO THE SPIRITS OF THE DEAD
For Claudia Crysis
she lived
90 years
her heirs
took care to set this up

The letterforms are confidently carved with good spacing, though the V in CLAVDIAE has been inserted afterwards to correct a spelling error. Although plain, some flourish is added by the use of ivy leaf interpuncts to separate the words. The deceased is named as Claudia Crysis. She is not identified by any specific role or indeed, through any of the usual adjectives we have seen used to memorialise women. In fact, we find out very little about Claudia beyond her name and her rather remarkable age: she lived until she was 90 years old. This is the oldest age recorded for a woman in Roman Britain although of course it is wholly unverifiable – especially when it had been so long removed from its original accompanying human remains. We're told in the final two lines that her heirs (plural) were responsible for erecting the monument, though their relationship to the deceased is not clarified beyond that. Had this ancient woman lived to 90, she may well have long outlived any children – or even grandchildren – of her own.

Chapter 5

Children

Over fifty of the surviving tombstones from Roman Britain belong to children. High infant mortality is a common feature of premodern societies, and the Roman Empire was certainly no different. Estimates suggest that almost 30 per cent of infants perished during the first year of their lives. Preterm, full-term and perinatal skeletons have been uncovered at a number of sites across Roman Britain, and the number of ancient infant remains recovered is vastly higher than the number of tombstones. Opinion is divided on the reason behind this: some argue it is evidence of Roman indifference towards young infants, some claim it indicates a prevalence of infanticide, while others take a more measured approach in highlighting that these findings simply indicate a different funerary ritual for this particular age group. It is difficult to point with certainty to any one explanation. But it is perhaps useful to highlight some of the recorded Roman practices and attitudes around the death of the very youngest children before turning to look at some of the tombstones themselves.

In the majority of cases, babies who died within the first six or so months of their lives were not cremated, which was the prevalent Roman funerary practice for disposing of a body in Roman Britain in the first and second centuries AD. Instead, we find more evidence of intramural burial for these infants: this means they were buried under or beside domestic buildings – something that was usually strictly forbidden for any other type of human remains. Roman funerary laws stipulated that any children who were over 6 years old at the time of their death would be officially mourned for a year, the same duration as an adult. Children under 6 years old at the time of their death were mourned for a month, while some report that infants less than a year old did not warrant an official mourning period at all. Pliny the Elder, a natural historian, noted that an infant was not considered a person in and of itself until six months had passed and they began to pass developmental milestones like teething, walking and talking.[1] Ideas like this were likely drawn from earlier Ancient Greek investigations into the early stages of life: the philosopher and scientist Aristotle, for example, had declared that it took forty days after birth for a baby to fully develop into a human being. As such, early infant death was often not considered to be as much of a loss as that of an older child or an adult, for the infant had not yet fully become a person. An often-cited quote from Roman politician and orator Cicero allegedly recommends that the death of an infant should not be a cause for grief or mourning:

> If a small child dies, the loss must be borne calmly; if an infant in the cradle, there must not event be a lament.[2]

But is it as straightforward as it seems? Caution is needed when lifting catchy quotes out of a larger text: this line, for example, comes from the *Tusculan Disputations*, a philosophical series of books written by Cicero following the sudden death of his adult daughter Tullia. In the passage in question, Cicero is addressing common beliefs around death, including the concept of 'dying before your time' – a concept that he takes issue with. It is within this criticism that our catchy quote appears as something that *other people say* when faced with a life cut so short it barely had time to start. Take a look at the line in question again, this time within a fuller extract of the passage:

> Let such absurdities as it being thought wretched to die before our time be considered as a sort of old wives' tale. What 'time', anyway? Nature's? It is she, after all, who has granted the use of life like a loan, without setting a repayment date. So what is there to complain about if she asks for it back whenever she wishes? You accepted the loan under these conditions. The same people think that if a small child dies, the loss must be borne calmly; if an infant in the cradle, there must not even be a lament. But in this latter case, Nature has recalled her gift with greater cruelty.[3]

Rather than advocating for a strictly unfeeling approach to infant death, Cicero here instead records the opinions of others – in a fairly critical tone – and if anything, describes the death of the youngest children as an especially harsh act of Nature herself. What we can take away from the discussion is that some Romans were certainly of the opinion that young children and babies did not warrant mourning, as by their reckoning they had not really started their lives yet. But was Cicero among them? As a follower of Stoic philosophy, he would not have endorsed excessive displays of grief over any individual death at any age. But there is nothing here to support the often-cited idea that Cicero specifically advised against grieving for younger children, on the basis of their age alone.

Another adherent to the Stoic way of life was Seneca the Younger, a politician and philosopher who lived during the reign of – and even acted as advisor to – the infamous Emperor Nero. In letters to friends and acquaintances, Seneca often tackles the subject of bereavement. He imparts stern advice to Marullus, who has recently lost his young son and has, in Seneca's view, been overindulging in his grief. Sticking to Stoic principles would provide the strength to deal with the death of this little child who was better known to his nurse than his father, Seneca notes. He repeatedly reminds Marullus that a moderate amount of tears and mourning is acceptable when someone dies, but these emotions should then be transformed into remembrance rather than continued grief. After all, he argues, in the grand scheme of things, aren't all our lives short?

Given the evidence drawn from the literary accounts, Roman attitudes towards infant death are often interpreted as harsh or indifferent by modern readers. But it is important to keep in mind that the ideas recorded within these texts are by no means representative of everyone living within the vast Roman Empire. The handful of opinions from elite male Roman writers does not offer us an insight into the thoughts and feelings of wider social classes, or the different cultures subsumed into the empire, or indeed the women who endured these pre-modern pregnancies and risked their own lives to give birth.

A COFFIN

The youngest recorded death from the surviving epitaphs across Roman Britain is that of Simplicia Florentina, an infant from Eboracum (York).[4] Her epitaph does not actually appear on a tombstone: instead, it is inscribed neatly on the side of her 1.2-metre-long stone sarcophagus. This was discovered in 1838 during excavations for the North Eastern Railway. A stone coffin like this would have been placed within a structure above ground rather than immediately buried, allowing the inscription to be read. Skeletal remains set in gypsum were discovered inside this coffin when it was excavated, but they did not belong to Simplicia. The bones *did* belong to a child but they were older than ten months. This tells us that the coffin had been recycled at a later date – a common occurrence with many coffins. What happened to Simplicia's remains is unknown.

The epitaph is composed of four uniformly carved lines followed by a short addendum in a less skilled hand.

<table>
<tr><th>Inscription</th><th>Expanded Text</th></tr>
<tr><td>D M SIMPLICIAE FLORENTINE</td><td>Dis Manibus Simpliciae Florentin(a) e</td></tr>
<tr><td>ANIME INNOCENTISSIME</td><td>anim(a) e innocentissim(a) e</td></tr>
<tr><td>QVE VIXIT MENSES DECEM</td><td>qu(a) e vixit menses decem</td></tr>
<tr><td>FELICIVS SIMPLEX > PATER FECIT</td><td>Felicius Simplex pater fecit</td></tr>
<tr><td>LEG VI V</td><td>legionis VI victricis</td></tr>
</table>

Translation
TO THE SPIRITS OF THE DEAD
For Simplicia Florentina
a most innocent soul
who lived 10 months
her father Felicius Simplex
centurion of the Victorious 6th Legion
made this

Simplicia was only ten months old when she passed away, yet her family chose to commemorate her in a more formal way than was perhaps expected. Simplicia herself is described as *anima innocentissima* ('a most innocent soul'), underscoring her short life. *Anima* was a common Latin term used for the soul: an animating life force inside the individual, which departed the body at the point of death. In popular belief, the soul would then journey to the underworld to face punishment or reward depending on the life it had led in the upper world. Simplicia's young soul is pointedly described as *innocentissima*, the superlative adjective here reinforcing her innocence: she was afforded neither the time nor opportunity to fully participate in the complex morality of life and as such her soul remains unblemished.

Her father's name – Felicius Simplex – is recorded as the dedicator. Just before the word *pater* on the inscription is a small roughly carved mark indicating that he was a centurion. This corresponds to the added note underneath naming the Victorious Sixth Legion as his unit. Felicius Simplex would thus have been a Roman citizen, as would his daughter. The details of his army post were evidently considered important enough to have been added in at some point after the original inscription, perhaps to more clearly identify the deceased and her paternal link to the area in which her memorial stood. Her mother is not mentioned on the epitaph.

A FATHER'S LAMENT

On another tombstone fragment from Eboracum lies an exceptional inscription, almost hiding in plain sight.[5] It was recovered in 1861 near to the site of the city's former Roman cemetery. Erected in memory of a young girl called Corellia Optata, the damaged gritstone with its slightly haphazard lettering may, at first glance, look fairly unremarkable. The top sculpture is now lost: we can see only the remains of two small feet, indicating that the inscription was once originally accompanied by a large portrait, likely a representation of the deceased herself. The letter D of the customary funerary abbreviation D M is lost on the left-hand side, though we can still see the accompanying M placed in its own circular frame on the opposite side.

The inscription is set within a moulded panel, with decorative shaping along the corners and the border. The irregular spacing of the lettering suggests that the lines were retrofitted into an existing frame, rather than planned out from the start, which likely indicates the purchase of a generic prefabricated tombstone rather than the commissioning of an individual bespoke design. In addition to recording the expected information like name of the deceased and age at time of death, ten of the lines also commemorate Corellia's life – and lament her early death – in poetic verse. These lines when taken together are written dactylic hexameter, the recognisable sound pattern of ancient epics like Homer's *Iliad* and *Odyssey* in Greek or Virgil's *Aeneid* in Latin.

Inscription
[D] M
CORELLIA OPTATA AN XIII
SECRETI MANES QVI REGNA
ACHERVSIA DITIS INCOLI
TIS QVOS PARVA PETVNT POST
LVMINA VITE EXIGVVS CINIS ET
SIMVLACRVM CORPOIS VM
BRA INSONTIS GNATE GENI
TOR SPE CAPTVS INIQVA
SVPREMVM HVNC NATE
MISERANDVS DEFLEO FINEM
Q CORE FORTIS PAT F C

Expanded Text with verse
Dis Manibus
Corellia Optata annorum XIII
Secreti Manes, qui regna Acherusia Ditis
incolitis, quos parua petunt post lumina uitae
exiguus cinis et simulacrum, corporis umbra
insontis gnatae genitor spe captus iniqua
supremum hunc natae miserandus defleo finem
Quintus Corellius Fortis pater faciendum curavit.

Translation
To the spirits of the dead
Corellia Optata 13 years old
You hidden spirits who dwell in Pluto's Acherusian
kingdom! You for whom the little ashes and the ghost –
shadow of the body – now search, after the brief light of life!
I, father of an innocent child, pitiable prisoner of unfair hope,
mourn my daughter's dying end.
Quintus Corellius Fortis, her father, set this up.

Corellia's tombstone has been set up by her father, Quintus Corellius Fortis. His age and occupation are not provided, though some have suggested he may have been an exemplary soldier who has earned the name 'Fortis' – an adjective meaning brave or strong – for his actions, perhaps another member of the Sixth Legion like the father from the previous epitaph. Corellia's cognomen 'Optata' does not derive from her father's given *tria nomina*: it may be linked to her mother, who is not named here, or it may simply be an alternative cognomen given to differentiate her from other Corellias within the family tree. 'Optata' is an interesting choice as it has the meaning 'wished for', leading some to wonder if this was bestowed upon her by parents who had long awaited her arrival into the world.[6]

The poetic lines of the inscribed verse offer a sharp contrast between life and death, while also underscoring the pain of a parent burying a child. Compositionally, this part of the inscription resembles an ancient prayer. Prayer was arguably the most common method of divine interaction in the ancient world. A formal prayer would usually begin with an invocation (*invocatio*) to the divine, which would not only address the god directly by name but also list where they reside and describe their general remit. It would then move on to the argument (*pars epica*), which would provide more context about the supplicant and their situation.

Here, the father addresses the spirits of the dead twice – first in the customary *Dis Manibus* formula, but then again more directly in the third line. He calls them 'hidden' spirits, as they are not the type of gods to regularly frequent the upper world; instead, they stay down in the murky depths of the underworld, where they are usually inaccessible to the living. Pluto is the god of the underworld and rules over it as his domain. 'Acherusian' emphasises this subterranean swampy location, as Acherusia was the name of one of the many lakes within the underworld itself. From the time of the Greek philosopher Plato into the Christian tradition, the Acherusian lake took on the specific purpose of cleansing the souls of the dead, enabling them to proceed onwards on their afterlife journeys.

The verse does not shy away from describing how Corellia herself has been transformed in death: her body is affectingly described as nothing more than a little pile of ashes, while her soul has departed onwards as a *simulacrum*, a spirit or ghost, described as a shadow of the body. This unusually direct funereal statement on the fate of the body and soul highlights the core

Fig. 5.1 Tombstone of Corellia Optata, on display at the Yorkshire Museum in York.

ancient Graeco-Roman belief that something survives the death of the physical body: something that represents the person, continues to resemble them, but is insubstantial in form. We find this idea expressed even in the earliest Ancient Greek poetry. In Homer's *Iliad*, the great epic set during the final year of the Trojan War, the warrior Achilles is visited by the ghost of his beloved cousin Patroclus. As Achilles tries to embrace Patroclus, his ghostly form is described as disappearing away beneath the earth like smoke, squeaking and gibbering as it goes. Achilles exclaims that even after death, a soul – an image of the person – survives, though it does not have any life left in it. Here, we find Corellia's post-mortem existence framed in the same way: a ghostly form resembling her in appearance but without any of the physicality of life.

The brevity of Corellia's young life is lamented throughout the short verse. We know from the initial line that she lived for only thirteen years, and her youth is emphasised throughout the lines that follow: she experienced only the brief (*parva*) light of life and is described as *insons*, 'a wholly innocent child'. Most poignantly, her cremated remains are described as *exiguus* – 'meagre' or 'scant' – which starkly evidences the small physical body she left behind. This is evocatively matched by the discovery of a glass vessel alongside the tombstone during excavations. Inside the vessel were cremated remains.

Missing from the prayer format of the lament is one key feature: the request. Here instead we find the father's grief at the finality of the situation. There is nothing he can do now but weep for his daughter. The vital essence of Corellia has departed onwards to the next world and cannot return. There is no request, only an end – and this is emphasised by the placement of *finem* ('end') at the end of the poem itself. This finality is visually matched by the poem's location on Corellia's tombstone, inscribed underneath the figure of a small girl, marking her final resting place in this world.

GREETINGS FOR A GOOD CHILD

In the nineteenth century, restoration work on a church near the site of Verteris fort (modern-day Brough, in Cumbria) led to the rediscovery of a comparatively small tombstone from the third century AD. Measuring around 33 centimetres wide by 58 centimetres tall, the stone had been reused as building material and suffered some damage to the left and lower edges in the process. Although there is no portrait or relief accompanying the stone, it has a striking appearance: between two vertical leafy borders are twelve densely written lines of Ancient Greek.[7]

The tombstone is dedicated to a 16-year-old boy called Hermes. Hermes is the name of the Ancient Greek messenger god who himself acts as a psychopomp – he helps guide souls on their way to the underworld. Like Corellia's inscription, rather than adopt the standard Roman format, we find a poetic commemoration written across five lines of dactylic – epic – hexameters. But unlike Corellia's Latin lament, Hermes' tombstone follows an older Ancient Greek epitaphic tradition in which a conversation takes place between the tombstone and the passer-by.

Inscription	Translation
ΕΚΚΑΙΔΕΧΕΤΗ ΤΙΣ	For anyone who happens to see
ΙΔΩΝ ΤΥΜΒΩ ΣΚΕΦΘΕΝΤ	Hermes, sixteen, of Commagene.
ΥΠΟ ΜΟΙΡΗΣ ΕΡΜΗ	Taken to his grave so young
ΚΟΜΜΑΓΗΝΟΝ ΕΠΟΣ	By Fate's plan all along.
ΦΡΑΣΑΤΩ ΤΟΔ ΟΔΕΙΤΗΣ ΧΑΙΡΕ ΣΥ	Here are the words to say
ΠΑΙ ΠΑΡ ΕΜΟΥ	As you pass him on your way:
ΚΗΝΠΕΡ ΘΝΗΤΟΝ ΒΙΟ	'Greetings child, from me to you
ΕΡΠΗΣ ΩΚΥΤΑΤ ΕΠ	Though this mortal life you're through.
ΤΗΣ ΓΑΡ ΜΕΡΟΠΩΝ ΕΠΙ	You've fluttered on, swift as can be,
ΚΙΜΜΕΡΙΩΝ ΓΗ[Ν] ΚΟΥ ΨΕΥ	To the land of Cimmerians over the sea.'
ΣΕΙ ΑΓ[ΑΘΟΣ] ΓΑΡ Ο ΠΑΙΣ ΡΕΞΕΙΣ	Do not cheat him but do this good deed,
ΔΕ ΣΥ [ΚΑΛΟΝ][8]	for he was a good child indeed.

The identity of whoever set up the stone is not revealed, nor is their relationship to Hermes made clear. We are told, however, that Hermes came from a place called Commagene. Located in modern-day south-east Turkey, Commagene has a long history: at the beginning of the first millennium BC, the area was ruled by the Neo-Hittites, then it was annexed by the Assyrians in 708 BC, followed by the Babylonians in the late seventh century BC. From the sixth century BC, it became a province of the Achaemenid Empire, and this lasted until Alexander the Great's conquest of the Persian Empire in the 330s BC. As a result, Commagene becomes 'Hellenised' – i.e. there is an influx of Greek language and culture across the conquered territories. Following the death of Alexander, Commagene falls under the control of the Seleucids. A revolt in 163 BC leads to independence and the kingdom of Commagene resists outside control for nearly 200 years. A fairly turbulent pattern of interactions with the Roman Empire then follow. Initially, under the emperor Tiberius (AD 17), it was annexed and became a Roman province. Then, under Caligula (AD 34), it regained its independence with Antiochus IV installed as king – only to lose it again shortly afterwards. Claudius later restored the kingdom once more under Antiochus IV (AD 41), but then, under Vespasian (AD 72), it was subsumed back into the Roman Empire as part of the ancient province of Syria.

Hermes himself has had a long journey from Commagene to Verteris. Verteris was situated on a ridge along the northern stretch of road that connected Eboracum and Luguvalium (Carlisle). To the east of the fort was the *vicus* (civilian settlement) and cemetery. Perhaps Hermes, like Victor in Chapter 3, was brought to the edge of the empire with the army as a slave in service to a soldier – this could explain the lack of familial detail on the tombstone, and the affection for him as a 'good child' worthy of acknowledgement. Or perhaps he belonged to a family from Commagene who had travelled across the Roman Empire for trade, and their choice of memorialisation reflects their Hellenised roots rather than their conformity to Roman custom. Whatever the case may be, Hermes has been thoughtfully remembered by those who were with him when he died. The choice to commemorate him in a Greek style and in the Greek language – which most passers-by would have not been able to read – firmly states his identity despite his resting place being in the far-flung reaches of northern Britannia.

The inscription on the tombstones addresses anyone passing by and proceeds to give instructions for greeting Hermes, acknowledging both his mortal resting place and his journey on to the underworld. His spirit has been able to flutter away quickly onwards. Many of the earliest descriptions of soul in Ancient Greek poetry describe it as something incorporeal and wispy, which flits or flies – sometimes even squeaking as it goes.[9] The tombstone also mentions the land of the Cimmerians as Hermes' post-mortem destination. This is an association that also stretches back as far as Homer. In the *Odyssey*, the long-suffering Odysseus must venture to the underworld as part of his travels. The directions he is given by the goddess and witch Circe direct him to the land of the Cimmerians, a place far across the sea that is continually shrouded in darkness.[10] Here, Odysseus and his men ultimately reach the entrance to the underworld: a destination Odysseus and Hermes of Commagene share.

INDIVIDUAL PORTRAITS

VACIA

In a cemetery just outside the Roman city of Luguvalium stood the tombstone of a little girl called Vacia.[11] The red sandstone monument was uncovered during excavations in 1885, facing upwards, alongside animal bones and two human skulls. The tombstone was originally discovered in one piece – until an unfortunate accident with a cart:

> A cart passed over it and broke off the top of the stone, which was at once knocked into fragments, and either built into foundations or pitched away—at any rate, it cannot be found.[12]

Roughly half of the tombstone features a full-length portrait set within a recess, though the damage to the top part of the monument left the figure without a head. Underneath the figure is an ansate panel, which features a short inscription.

Inscription	Expanded Text
DIS	*Dis [Manibus]*
VACIA INF	*Vacia infans*
ANS AN III	*annorum III*

Translation
TO THE SPIRITS OF THE DEAD
Baby Vacia
3 years old

Vacia's young age is emphasised by the Latin word *infans*, the root of our own English 'infant'. We are given no other information about her, and do not know who has set up the stone. The letter carving on the inscription is confident and well spaced, if a little haphazard. The figure on the tombstone is carved in great detail, and although the head is missing it is clear that the age of the pictured girl does not quite match up to the 3-year-old Vacia as described in the inscription. This could suggest that this was originally a prefabricated tombstone that came with a figure already carved when it was purchased and a blank panel for adding the details of the deceased.[13] Or it may well be a matter of artistic preference: children are often represented as miniature adults in ancient art rather than in their infant form.

Little Vacia is dressed well for the northern reaches of Britannia. She wears a long tunic that falls in folds and reaches all the way down to her feet. Over the tunic is a thick belted cloak, with long sleeves gathered just past the elbow. A bundle of fabric is swept around the neck and chest, too. The amount of cosy clothing Vacia is dressed in led Ferguson to suppose the child 'died of bronchitis'[14] – an interesting, if unknowable, assertion! She is holding an object in her right hand, though through wear over the centuries its precise details are difficult to discern: it has been variously identified as a fir cone or a bunch of grapes – perhaps a favourite snack of the deceased, remembered on her monument. Grapes were, after all, one of the many foods brought to the province by the Romans. Or it may inhabit a less literal symbolism, as grapes are often shown held by women or children on funerary monuments from elsewhere in the empire, perhaps representing in some way an untimely death. [15]

PERVICA

Out along Hadrian's Wall again, near the fort site of Aesica (Great Chesters), we come face to face with another young girl. Roughly two thirds of this 1.6-metre high monument is taken up by a depiction of a small figure standing within a niche.[16] Underneath is a recessed panel with space for the inscription, though interestingly on this example, letters have also been carved in the small area above the panel. Decorative elements have also been added to above and around the arch of the recess, including swirls and zigzag lines. The full panel space for the inscription has not been used.

Inscription
DIS M
PERVICAE FILIAE

Expanded Text
Dis Manibus
Pervicae filiae

Translation
TO THE SPIRITS OF THE DEAD
For [my] daughter Pervica

The design of the tombstone is plain but striking nonetheless: the figure looks out at the viewer, her face rounded and childlike with simple features marked out on the stone. Her hair is short and curled around her forehead, and she is dressed comfortably in a loose long-sleeved tunic, which hangs down past her knees and simple boots. Her arms rest in front of her – the right is slightly raised, hinting that perhaps she once held an object. She looks around the same age as the girls from Coria – though as we have seen in other examples, the portraiture may not always be an accurate reflection of age.

We have no further details in the inscription for Pervica – her age is not given, nor is the name of whoever set up the stone. The space left underneath the single line on the inscription panel suggests that these details were intended to be added later. The customary *Dis Manibus* abbreviation has been carved less neatly into the thin space between the niche and the panel, suggesting a later addition by a different hand. This is an interesting example of memorialisation for a child: the parents or relatives who erected it evidently went to great lengths to ensure Pervica was remembered by commissioning this little portrait. The limited information provided through the inscription suggests that for them, perhaps, the visual representation on the stone held much more significance than any lettering.

AN UNKNOWN CHILD

Part of a tombstone recovered near the site of Brocavum (Brougham) shows a figure of a small child within a stepped recess.[17] Although the top of the tombstone has been lost – likely when the stone was later reused in construction of a weir on the river Eamont – some of the figure and the lower section of inscription remain clear.

Inscription

[...]
ANNAMORIS PATER
ET RESSONA MATER
F C

Expanded Text

[...]
Annamoris pater
et Ressona mater
faciendum curaverunt

Translation

[...]
Annamoris his father
and Ressona his mother
set this up

The figure on the tombstone is missing the head. From the size and shape of the remaining body, it seems reasonable to identify it as a child, and indeed the accompanying inscription naming both parents supports this interpretation. The names of the parents – Annamoris and Ressona – are rather noticeably un-Roman in origin, yet here they are in a Latin inscription. These particular names have been described as 'unabashedly barbarian' and are included in the *Celtic Personal Names of Roman Britain* database.[18]

The child is bundled up in a thick cloak. An illustration from 1875 records more detail than can be seen on the object now: the child's cloak is draped in V-shaped folds below the neck in the style of a *paenula*. The *paenula* was an outer garment popular with travellers especially in wet or cold weather; rather than draping around the shoulders, it fitted over the head (similar to a poncho) and hung loosely around the body. This type of cloak was usually made from thick wool, though some Roman writers also mention a leather version (*paenula scortea*). The child's left arm is raised, and in his hand he holds a small circular object – or, at least, there is a circular-shaped space for whatever object was held in the hand. Perhaps a small pet – a bird – or a toy. Two small little legs support the body, though no footwear is visible.

A LITTLE CHARIOTEER

On a September morning in 1828, not far from Voreda (Old Penrith) fort, workmen discovered a red sandstone tombstone that had been buried face-down in the ground. It had miraculously survived intact and measured over

2.2 metres tall by just under 1 metre wide.[19] Other inscribed stone fragments and funerary urns – still containing their ashes – were discovered along with the tombstone. On pulling it from the ground, they came face to face with a young boy. His full-body portrait stands within a rectangular recess and occupies over half of the stone's surface. The top of the stone is gabled with some small rosette decoration to the upper points. The inscription sits beneath the figure within a rectangular panel. The lettering is undamaged.

<table>
<tr><td align="center">Inscription</td><td align="center">Expanded Text</td></tr>
<tr><td align="center">DIS</td><td align="center">Dis Manibus</td></tr>
<tr><td align="center">MANIB M COCCEI</td><td align="center">Marci Coccei</td></tr>
<tr><td align="center">NONN ANNOR VI</td><td align="center">Nonni annorum VI</td></tr>
<tr><td align="center">HIC SITUS EST</td><td align="center">hic situs est</td></tr>
</table>

Translation
TO THE SPIRITS OF THE DEAD
for Marcus Cocceius Nonnus
6 years old
here he lies

The arrangement of the epitaph is a little unusual as the first word – DIS – sits alone on the first line, centred and in a larger size, while the abbreviated MANIB is placed at the beginning of the second line in smaller lettering. The full(ish) appearance of the phrase points to an early date during the first century AD. The lettering itself is slightly irregular at times. Ligatures have been used (IB, NI), there is some overwriting of the double N in Nonnus, and the EI which ends the second line has been added in much smaller letters, suggesting the stonemason had either run out of space or added it in afterwards. The I letterforms stand larger than the rest in DIS and HIC, an epigraphic habit that dates the monument to the end of the first century or early years of the second century AD.[20]

Following the dedication to the spirits of the dead, we are given the name of the deceased: Marcus Cocceius Nonnus. The fairly traditional *tria nomina* indicates that the child was a Roman citizen. Birley discusses how the child's name here may possibly offer us a date for the monument: male children were usually named after their father, and if this was the case here, the name indicates that the father had received citizenship under the emperor Nerva, taking both his praenomen (Marcus) and nomen (Cocceius) as a result.[21] Given the remote northern location, it seems likely that the citizenship would have been granted to the father for his service as an auxiliary soldier. Fortunately for us, Nerva had a notably short reign as emperor from AD 96 to 98. This means that AD 96 is the earliest possible date for citizenship to have been conferred upon the father and subsequently on any of his existing children – meaning that for the child to bear this name on the tombstone, it could not have been erected before this.

Nonnus' age at the time of death is recorded as 6 years old. We are not given any further information about his family or the dedicator of the monument; instead, we have one of the customary funerary phrases added at the end – here he lies (*hic situs est*). This, too, suggests a date towards the earlier half of the Roman occupation of Britain, as it gradually fell out of use over time.

Fig. 5.2 Illustration of the tombstone of Marcus Cocceius Nonnus.

Nonnus himself is shown standing within the recess, his feet resting comfortably over the bottom frame. He is dressed in a loose and bulky sleeved cloak – possibly another example of the Gallic coat – and wears a scarf wrapped closely around his neck. He did have, at one point, small soft boots on his feet. The face has been damaged though some details of the features are just about still discernible: two large rounded eyes sit closely together, suggesting a rather Celtic-influenced style of carving the portrait. The hair is brushed back neatly away from the face and behind the ears, which are still visible on each side. Nonnus raises a palm branch with his right hand while on the left he clutches a whip across the front of his body. These are symbols of the victorious chariot racer (*auriga*) – the palm branch being awarded to the winner of the race. At 6 years old, Nonnus may be a little too young to compete in the chariot races but it is strikingly modern to think that these objects have been added here instead to memorialise this little boy's favourite entertainment – or perhaps even reflect his own future aspirations. While only one chariot-racing course (known as a *circus*) has been found in the province – a large 8,000-seater venue in Camulodunum (Colchester) – there would likely have been smaller races held elsewhere for entertainment, albeit in more modest surroundings.

THREE GIRLS FROM CORIA

In the far northern Roman town of Coria or Coriosopitum (modern-day Corbridge) near Hadrian's Wall, three separate tombstones have been recovered for three little girls.[22] Carved from buff sandstone, two have survived in good condition while one is fragmentary. The two unbroken monuments were discovered face-down in the ground, having been reused in a later period as paving stones. Both feature a carved figure in a niche with an inscription underneath. The fragmented piece retains the inscription only.

The first of these tombstones is dedicated to a 5-year-old girl known as Ahteha. The full inscription on her memorial reads as follows:

Inscription	**Expanded Text**
DM	*Dis Manibus*
AHTEHE	*Ahtehe*
FIL NOBILIS	*filia Nobilis*
VIXIT ANIS V	*vixit annos V*

Translation
TO THE SPIRITS OF THE DEAD
Ahteha
daughter of Nobilis
she lived for 5 years

The small carved figure has worn away, leaving just the shape of the upper body and head. Small outlines can be seen for the nose and arms. Given the rough texture of the stone, it is likely that the figure was plastered and then painted when it was created. The script of the inscription is large and effusive, with sweeping ligatures on several letters. The shape of the A in the second line is particularly unusual – mirroring the elaborate M in the line above it – with the long flourish on the downstroke creating a letterform almost like the lambda of the Ancient Greek alphabet, especially when compared to use of the lambda letterform for L on Successa Petronia's epitaph. The stylistic and confident strokes suggest an experienced stonemason, and have been cited as an argument against possible spelling mistakes in the given name, which is most commonly read as Ahteha.

Ahteha is an intriguing name for this little girl living on the very edge of the empire. It is not a typical Roman name, but then we find many non-Roman names transcribed on tombstones across the province. In the extensive discussion of this name, which accompanies the original excavation reports by Birley from 1938, Gutenbrunner argues that Ahteha, and the inscription's dative form

Fig. 5.3 Tombstone of Ahteha, on display at Corbridge Roman fort and museum.

Ahteh(a)e, retains a Germanic *-ehae* ending found in *Matronae* names in the Rhineland.[23] Taken along with the *Aht-* stem, which Gutenbrunner sees as a likely derivation from Old Germanic vocabulary, he suggests that Ahteha is a pet name derived from a Germanic compound word. Names are generally more susceptible to linguistic interference and can often be distorted by changes to the spelling or word form as well as hypocorism – the use of a nickname. This could be a shortened version of the existing name or something entirely unrelated, and is often used as a means of expressing affection. We see this on the second tombstone, too, for a little girl known as Ertola.

Ertola's monument stands at just over 1.5 metres tall. Unlike Ahteha's, the carved figure in the niche is much larger and survives in much better condition. It is a basic but charming figure of a child dressed in a warm tunic, belted at the waist, which falls down past her knees. Her feet have been broken off at some point. Her hands hold a prized object before her: a ball. It is a poignant scene, the young deceased child eternally holding a favourite toy, yet poor Ertola's figure has found itself the subject of much criticism in scholarship for its non-classical style. Scholars have focused witheringly on her 'hunched' shoulders to her 'spindly' legs, and the altogether 'primitive' manner of carving. But rather than evaluate its worth based on its proximity to classical sculpture, it is perhaps more worthwhile to reflect on what this stone might tell us about who lived in and around Hadrian's Wall. Ertola's figure is carved in the Celtic style, like many objects discovered in Roman Corbridge. Yet she is also accompanied by a Latin inscription that follows the standard Roman funerary formulae.

The inscription panel sits underneath the figure. It is smaller and less clear than Ahteha's inscription, and it seems that at some point, an existing inscription was erased then Ertola's memorial was added on top.

Fig. 5.4 Tombstone of Ertola, on display beside Ahteha at Corbridge Roman fort and museum.

Inscription	**Expanded Text**
D M	*Dis Manibus*
SVDRENVS	*Sudrenus*
ERTOLE NOMINE	*Ertole nomine*
VELLIBIA FELICISSI	*Vellibia felicissime*
ME VIXIT ANIS IIII	*vixit annos IIII*
DIEBVS LX	*diebus LX*

Translation

TO THE SPIRITS OF THE DEAD
Sudrenus set this up
for Ertola, also called Vellebia
she lived most happily for 4 years
and 60 days

We discover from the inscription that Ertola's monument has been set up by her father, Sudrenus. She is also given a second, more formal, name, Vellebia. These names are included in the *Celtic Personal Names of Roman Britain* database, and combined with the style of tombstone certainly suggest an ancient Celtic family unit – though one that has adapted to Roman customs and language for the commemoration of their dead. The inscription adds in the detail *felicissime* ('most happily') before *vixit* ('she lived'), letting the tombstone's viewer know that Ertola had the happiest life, even if it was a short one.

The third fragmentary tombstone has no surviving decoration, but the inscription is still legible.

<table>
<tr><td align="center">Inscription</td><td align="center">Expanded Text</td></tr>
<tr><td align="center">IVLIA MATE[.]</td><td align="center">Julia Materna</td></tr>
<tr><td align="center">NA AN VI IVL</td><td align="center">annos VI Julius</td></tr>
<tr><td align="center">MARCELLINVS</td><td align="center">Marcellinus</td></tr>
<tr><td align="center">FILIAE CARISSIMAE</td><td align="center">filiae carissimae</td></tr>
</table>

Translation
Julia Materna
6 years old
Julius Marcellinus set this up
for his dearest daughter

The breaks in the stone render the final letter of the first line entirely unreadable, hence the square brackets in the transcription. Luckily, it is clear that we have just a single letter gap in the middle of a female name, so it is unlikely to be anything other than the 'Materna'. Julia's tombstone has been set up by her father, Julius Marcellinus. We are told that she lived for six years, and the father's loss is underscored by the addendum *filiae carissimae*. Interestingly, we find a Julius Marcellinus appearing a little further along Hadrian's Wall at Banna, modern-day Birdoswald. This site sits around 25 miles west of Corbridge, straddling the wall itself. On an altar to the god Jupiter, Julius Marcellinus is named as the centurion acting in command of the Second Legion Augusta in the dedicatory inscription.[24] Could it be the same man?

Note that, in contrast to the previous tombstones, we have two traditional Roman names appearing here following traditional naming patterns: Julia, as the daughter, takes the feminine form of her father's name, Julius. Julia's inscription panel does not include the standard abbreviation D M but that does not necessarily mean it was completely missing – sometimes we find these letters carved in upper sections of the stone. Another funerary fragment from Corbridge shows these letters placed above the space that holds the carved figure.

ENSLAVED CHILDREN

A neatly carved inscription on a tombstone from Deva (Chester) commemorates the lives of three young boys.[25] It stands at just over 1.3 metres tall and has been almost completely reconstructed, despite being broken into several fragments and reused in the building of Chester's north wall. The design on the tombstone is symmetrical if rather plain: there are no portraits of the boys themselves, and the decoration amounts to two rosettes (one now missing) and triangles above the inscription. But perhaps the most striking part of this memorial is that it was not set up by the boys' parents: instead, the stone tells us, it was erected by their *dominus* – their master – meaning these three boys were owned as slaves.

Inscription	Expanded Text
DIS MANIBVS	*Dis Manibus*
ATIL[.] E[.] N	*Atil[ianus] e[t]*
TIAT[.] LIANUS AN X	*[A] nt[i] atilianus annorum X*
PROTUS AN XII	*Protus annorum XII*
POMPEIUS	*Pompeius Optatus*
OPTATUS DO	*Dominus*
MINUS F C	*faciendum curavit*

Translation
TO THE SPIRITS OF THE DEPARTED
Atilianus and Antiatilianus
10 years old
and Protus
12 years old
Pompeius Optatus
their master
took care to set this up

The use of the term *Dis Manibus* on the inscription rather than the D M abbreviation suggests a date within the first century AD. The lettering here is mostly uniform and well spaced, with some use of interpuncts, and interesting ligatures at the beginning of the inscription: the DIS MANIBUS is an especially good example, with the M/A and N/I combined to ensure a balanced line.

The second and third lines have suffered the most damage, leaving the exact reading of the names recorded here rather difficult. Only the lower strokes remain of the rather puzzling E in the second line in particular; the depth and position suggest that the E was inscribed backwards and possibly formed part of a ligature (ET). Most editors reconstruct the lines as ATILIAN ET ANTIATILIANUS AN X, as followed above, which seems reasonable based on the rest of the inscription's spacing and ligatures. But why shorten the first name (Atilianus) and none of the others? A more recent suggestion of ATILIANE AN / I ATILIANUS AN X has been made by Alfody, and supported by Tomlin.[26] On this reading, the information recorded on the second and third lines would thus be:

Atiliane 1 year old
Atilianus 10 years old

This would then instead record the still similar names of two children, Atiliane, a very young infant, and Atilianus, a 10-year-old boy. The name Atiliane does not appear anywhere else, though as we have seen, there were often unique names recorded in Britannia so this cannot completely rule it out. If we follow the original reading, by comparison, we find two boys, Atilianus and Antiatilianus, who both passed away at the age of 10. The names along with their identical age at the time of death would suggest that they were twin brothers. In lines four and five we discover that the monument is also dedicated to a third child, a boy named Protus. He has died aged 12. What has led to the death of these three young, enslaved children from the same household? Alas, we are rarely given an insight into the cause of death on tombstones. Given the children's status as slaves, there are many ways in which they could have met their fate, whether by disease, accident or injury.

The young ages of the children (on either reading) may indicate that they were *vernae*: slaves who had been born into the household from a slave mother rather than purchased by the master. *Vernae* were considered slaves from birth and had no rights, but like their mother were the property of the master. These 'home-born' slaves were more valued than those that were bought on the open market as they were thought to be better behaved and more loyal; some formed closer bonds with their owners' families and could earn their freedom earlier than slaves brought in from the outside.[27]

We are given little other information about the three children except for the identification of their master as the one who has erected the monument. His name is recorded as Pompeius Optatus. We are not told what occupation or role he held, though within the Roman family unit he would certainly have been the *pater familias*, the head of the household. In this role, he was responsible for the enslaved members of the household as well as his family relations; as such, some view the erection of the tombstone for the children optimistically as a sign of his affection.[28] But the pessimist may say that the tombstone is ultimately more about Pompeius Optatus than the children: by commissioning such a monument to stand in the cemetery with his own name and relationship so plainly stated, it tells us more about how he wished to be seen by his social peers as a kind and benevolent (thus exemplary) master to the many slaves in his household.

Another tombstone from Glevum Colonia (Gloucester) provokes similar reflection on the relationship between slave and master in these memorials. Limestone fragments belonging to the tombstone of another young slave were recovered during excavation work in 2004.[29] The monument has fared poorly over the centuries: both the top and bottom sections are lost, and the surviving fragments have suffered extensive wear to the surface. It originally comprised a relief of the deceased set within a niche, below which was the inscription on plain stone without framing the usual recessed panel. In its day, the tombstone would have stood well over 1 metre tall.

<table>
<tr><td align="center">Inscription</td><td align="center">Expanded Text</td></tr>
<tr><td align="center">MARTIALIS</td><td align="center">Martialis</td></tr>
<tr><td align="center">C [..] LONI SERV[.]</td><td align="center">C. Ciloni servi</td></tr>
<tr><td align="center">[..] O XIIII</td><td align="center">anno XIIII</td></tr>
<tr><td align="center">[..] E</td><td align="center">hic situs est</td></tr>
</table>

Translation
For Martialis
slave of Gaius Cilonius
14 years old
here he lies

The monument has no dedication to the spirits of the dead, pointing to an early date of creation during the first century AD. The single name of the deceased is given first: this is a boy called Martialis, who is immediately then identified in the second line as the slave of a man called Gaius Cilonius. Martialis was 14 years old when he died. The monument records little else beyond the customary closing phrase 'here he lies' (*hic situs est*), which again points to an earlier date for its creation. It is a plain and straightforward epitaph: the deceased is memorialised by their name, their status, and their age at the time of death.

The relief that surmounted the inscription is still discernible despite its damage and wear. It shows a dining scene – another example of the *totenmahl* motif we have now seen many times. An adult male figure reclines on a central high-backed couch. He leans on his left side, his elbow resting on a plump cushion. He is dressed in the toga, which is draped over his head: the stonemason has taken care to show the folds of the fabric cascading down from the head and over the shoulders. The man has neatly styled hair, which sits around the crown of his head and reflects the Julio-Claudian style of portraiture popular in the middle of the first century AD.[30] In his left hand, he holds a large scroll in front of his chest. The usual three-legged table sits in front of the couch with a jug and a cup placed on the top. To the left of the scene is a second figure: he has been badly damaged but the head and feet remain intact, and from his smaller stature and position at the foot of the couch it is clear that he is the slave attending on his master – this, rather than the large well-dressed central adult figure, represents the deceased Martialis.

What does this say about the master, then, that he chose a monument in which he was the focus rather than the deceased? Even in death, Martialis does not escape his service: he is eternally attending on his master, who relaxes and enjoys the convivial dinner. Most conjecture that this was another example of a prefabricated tombstone: Gaius Cilonius had not commissioned the scene specifically but merely chosen it from a selection of existing options. Does this make it any less of a statement on the master/slave relationship? As with our pessimistic interpretation above, here we see much more visibly how the funerary monument could serve as a reflection of the dedicator. Rather than a memorial for the deceased child, the focus remains very much on Gaius Cilonius as the boy's master.

A FOSTER CHILD

A red sandstone monument from Voreda (Old Penrith) highlights another relationship that could exist between adult and child in the Roman world, as it records the death of a foster child called Hylas.[31] The tombstone was recovered at some point in the early nineteenth century near the triangular well at Old Penrith during work to improve the road. It remained at Lowther Castle until it was sold to the British Museum in 1969. The stone was broken into three large pieces: reassembled, it stands just over 1 metre tall. It is modestly decorated: a pediment to the top features a circle at its centre and the inscription sits underneath. It appears roughly carved and runs over seven lines in total.

Inscription

D M
YLAE ALVM
NI KARIS
SIMI VIXIT
AN XIII CL SE
VERVS TRIB
MILIT

Expanded Text

Dis Manibus
Ylae alum-
ni karis-
simi vixit
annos XIII Claudius Se-
verus tribunus
militum

Translation

TO THE SPIRITS OF THE DEAD
For Hylas
dearly beloved foster child
he lived 13 years
Claudius Severus
military tribune
(set this up)

Following the full abbreviation to the spirits of the dead (D M), we are given the name of the deceased in the dative case. The name is obviously written in the Latin alphabet here – YLAE, the dative form for YLAS. Rather than the name Ylas, this is likely meant to be the Greek name Hylas, which is written as Ὕλας in Greek script.[32] Hylas is identified by a single name only.

After his name, Hylas is immediately described as an *alumnus*, which is usually translated into English as a 'foster child'. This Latin title indicated a child who was not raised by their birth parents but was not legally adopted: the child could not claim any inheritance or adopt the name of their foster parents, or indeed enjoy any of the socio-cultural advantages of legally joining a family. Fostering was an informal arrangement in the Roman world: it usually involved children of a young age who were placed in the care of someone who was not a blood relative. These children may have been abandoned, sold by their parents, or found themselves orphaned. The most common form of fostering was basically a type of slavery, as the child would take on a servile role in the foster household.[33] Like the *vernae*, we see that many fostering relationships could nonetheless develop bonds of genuine affection. Here, Hylas is referred to using one of the terms of endearment we commonly see on graves for beloved family members –

especially wives and daughters – *karissimi* (dearly beloved). This choice of superlative could certainly emphasise the bond that existed between the deceased and the dedicator.

Hylus lived for thirteen years. We are given no other information about him beyond the name of his foster parent, a man called Claudius Severus. He is identified as a military tribune, which tells us that he was an important official within the army unit who ranked above the centurion. We are not given any further details on his origins or his military unit. Tomlin suggests he may have been a legionary officer commanding the detachment of the Twentieth Legion, who were attested at Voreda.[34] Despite Hylus' status as *alumnus*, Severus has erected this monument to ensure he is remembered in an affectionate way – and, like we see with the tombstones of slaves, record his own benevolence as foster parent.

FAMILY PORTRAITS

FLAVIA AUGUSTINA

Given the high infant mortality rate, it is not surprising that we often encounter more than one child commemorated on the same stone. A tombstone may also include one or both parents alongside their children – though in the majority of cases, the deceased parent is the mother. These memorials can offer a brief glimpse into the ideals of Roman family life.

Standing at just over 1.7 metres tall is the impressive tombstone for a woman called Flavia Augustina and her two children from the Roman provincial capital Eboracum.[35] Discovered during excavations at the Driffield Estate in 1859, the tombstone had actually been reused as the lid for a later coffin. The upper two thirds of the stone feature a detailed carving of four figures. The inscription panel occupies the lower third. On the stone's right side, the mason has carved images of his own tools including a hammer and a set square. The monument now stands on display in the Yorkshire Museum, where visitors are able to view this wonderful family portrait up close.

It is from the inscription that we learn this stone once marked the resting place of three of the four family members depicted.

Inscription

D M FLAVIAE AVGVSTINAE
VIXIT AN XXXVIIII M VII D XI FILIVS
SAENIVS AVGSTINVS VIXIT AN I D III
[...] A VIXIT AN I M VIIII D V G
AERESIVS
SAENVS VET LEG VI VIC CONIVGI
CARI
[.] SIMAE ET SIBI F C

Expanded Text

Dis Manibus Flaviae Augustinae
vixit annos XXXVIIII menses VII dies XI filius
Saenius Augustinus vixit annos I dies III
[...] a vixit annos I menses VIIII dies V
Gaius Aeresius Saenus veteranus
legionis VI Victricis coniugi
carissimae et sibi faciendum curavit

Translation

TO THE SPIRITS OF THE DEAD
For Flavia Augustina who lived 39 years, 7 months and 11 days
For Saenius Augustinus their son who lived 1 year and 3 days [...]
for their daughter who lived 1 year, 9 months and 5 days
Gaius Aeresius Saenus, veteran of the Victorious Sixth Legion,
set this up for his dearest wife and his own children

The tombstone has been set up by a man called Gaius Aeresius Saenus to mark the passing of his wife Flavia Augustina and two of their children – a son, called Saenius Augustinus, and a daughter whose name is no longer legible on the inscription. The lettering is fairly uniformly carved, though the naming of Flavia Augustina in the first line appears slightly larger than the lines that follow. The inscription is noticeably longer than many of the usual epitaphs, spanning a total of six lines within the panel. Spaces between most of the words are marked with interpuncts in the form of small

Fig. 5.5 Detail from the tombstone of Flavia Augustina and her two children, on display at the Yorkshire Museum, York.

dots. Ligatures appear occasionally for the letter combination AE, always for AN (here the consistent abbreviation for *annos* – 'years').

The epitaph provides an incredibly specific accounting of each family member's age at their time of death down to the number of days. This reads especially poignantly in the case of the two young children, emphasising the brevity of their lives: Saenius only just made it past his first birthday while his sister was not too far off her second. This level of detail also speaks to a level of care taken in commemorating the deceased. That Gaius can – quite literally – count the days he spent with his family is a way of very visibly representing his grief and loss, whether these final tallies are accurate or not.

Reading the inscription alongside the family portrait throws up an interesting puzzle. We are told both children were under 2 years old when they passed away. Yet, in their tombstone depiction, they appear much older. The depiction of children on Roman funerary monuments could often be aspirational, showing the children in their later stages of life all the way through to adulthood as a symbolic commemoration of their unfulfilled potential. Thus, the family's two young infants are here imagined as older children, taking on the dress and stance of their corresponding parent, much further along the path to becoming good Roman citizens themselves.

Flavia herself is shown as the tallest of the group, just edging above the figure of her husband. This too is slightly unusual: the scale of figures within a group carving often indicates their status, and so a married woman was typically represented as smaller in stature than her husband. The family are dressed in warm clothes – essential attire for Roman Britain. Flavia and her daughter wear thick cloaks draped around their chest and shoulders, which they hold in place with their raised right hand. Gaius and his son are dressed in the *paenula*, a heavy travel cloak. You can see on the tombstone how their cloak is draped differently with a long triangular or V-shaped drop of fabric to the front. Underneath the cloak, we can see all four family members are dressed in long tunics. All wear covered shoes on their feet.

Each family member also holds an object of some kind in their hands. Gaius clutches a scroll in his left hand, which some have interpreted as his discharge papers given his status as a *veteranus*. This detail would visibly emphasise his position as both an army veteran and a Roman citizen, neatly aligning the image with the information communicated in the inscription.

Flavia clutches something bulky in her raised right hand and holds out another object in her left hand. Different suggestions have been made for each – a scroll or vessel for the bulky object, and perhaps a bird for the smaller one. The children both hold round items in front of them – likely a ball, as we saw with Ahteha's tombstone above, emphasising their youthfulness and playful ages.

VITALIS

A gabled tombstone recovered from Onnum (Halton Chesters), one of the forts along Hadrian's Wall, preserves a rather elegant family portrait of two adults and a child.[36] They are positioned within a rectangular panel, three sides of which are decorated with a cabled frame. All three figures face the viewer. Although the top of the tombstone is missing, it is possible to see the remnants of a carved pinecone in the centre of the gable. As we saw with the tombstone of Aurelia Aureliana in Chapter 4, pinecones often appear in funerary contexts in the Roman world as their symbolism was linked to the cycle of death and rebirth.

Letters have been hastily carved on either side of the pinecone: VI to the left and TALIS squashed in to the right over two lines. The cuts are not made with the same precision as the main inscription, which sits beneath the portrait, suggesting it was added afterwards. Unfortunately, most of the main inscription on this one has now been lost as almost all of the lower section is missing. Some letters are still identifiable on the remainder of the lower right side.

Inscription	Expanded Text
VITA LIS	*Vitalis*
[D] M	*[Dis] Manibus*
[...] M POSV	*[titulum] posu-*
[...] IRILIS E	*[erunt V irilis et*
[...] S VI	*[...] s vi-*
[...] VO S	*[...s] uo s*
[...]	*[ibi...]*

Translation
Vitalis
TO THE SPIRITS OF THE DEAD
Virilis and [...] s
set up this tombstone
[for their son]
[...]

The three figures are well dressed in heavy draped cloaks: the mother's falls in the triangular 'V' shape around her chest, while the father's sits more like the *sagum*, a thick outer cloak fastened at his right shoulder. This suggests the father was perhaps a military man: as Tomlin notes, even fully intact inscriptions from military sites do not always explicitly mention military connections – especially those recovered from fort cemeteries.[37]

The mother's hair is gathered on the top of her head, a fashionable hairstyle for a Roman lady in the third century AD. The individual features beyond this are mostly worn away but it is clear to the viewer that the scene is one of familial affection: the two parents are positioned to the back, their heads slightly tilted inwards towards each other, and each parent rests a hand on the shoulder of the child positioned in front of them.

Fig. 5.6 Tombstone of Vitalis and family, on display at the Great North Museum: Hancock, Newcastle upon Tyne.

This composition, along with the bits and pieces of inscription we can recover, suggests the tombstone is for the child – the likeliest owner of the added name Vitalis.

MOTHER AND DAUGHTER

One of the many tombstones recovered from The Mount cemetery at Eboracum is dedicated to two females, thought to be mother and daughter.[38] Standing at just over 1.7 metres tall, the stone has been broken in two but both parts have survived in reasonably good condition. The upper section shows a portrait of an older woman and young child together, while the lower section preserves their information within a simple panel.

Inscription	Expanded Text
D M	*Dis Manibus*
IVLIE BRICE AN XXXI	*Julie Brice annos XXXI*
SEPRONIE MARTINE AN VI	*Sepronie Martine annos VI*
SEPRONIVS MARTINVS F C	*Sepronius Martinus faciendum curavit*

Translation
TO THE SPIRITS OF THE DEAD
For Julia Brica 31 years old
and for Sepronia Martina 6 years old
Sepronius Martinus set this up

The information provided is fairly minimal. We are told the names and ages of both of the deceased: Julia Brica died at the age of 31, while Sepronia Martina passed away at the age of 6. We are also given the name of the person who has set up the memorial, Sepronius Martinus. The relationship between the three is not explicitly stated but it seems very reasonable to assume that this is the wife and child of Sepronius, especially given the naming of the child after the father.

The upper section supports this interpretation. It shows two figures standing together within a niche. The smaller figure of Sepronia mirrors that of Julia. Both are dressed in elegantly draped tunic and cloak. Julia's hair is pulled back and gathered at the nape, while Sepronia wears her hair loose. Each figure holds an item to their left side, though the wear to the stone over the years makes it difficult to now discern the objects clearly. Julia clutches a large pottery vessel or a basket while Sepronia holds what looks like a small pet – likely a little bird.[39]

MOTHER AND SON

The two halves of this tombstone from Eboracum, dedicated to a mother and her young son, were reunited after more than 300 years apart.[40] The large rectangular limestone monument, wider than it is tall, had been broken into two pieces and recycled as building material for a church. The right section was used in the church's south wall, where it was spotted in the seventeenth century by Martin Lister. In a letter dated to 10 March 1683, he recorded the observation:

> A broken inscription in the church-wall of All Saints North Street, with the figure of a naked woman in bas relief on the left side of it. The letters (as many of them remain) are exceedingly fairly cut, beyond any thing I have yet seen of Roman antiquities in England, and the Stone of a finer grain than ordinary. It is a monument of conjugal affection.

Lister also recorded a small sketch of the inscription, noting the difficulty in discerning whether it was for a husband of a wife from the fragmentary text. This stone piece remained in place, exposed to the elements, until 1867, when it was relocated to the Yorkshire Museum. The left tombstone section was also used in the church's construction but proved to be more elusive. Having been used to underpin the north wall, it remained concealed and was not rediscovered until 1931. The two halves were finally reunited, and the inscription could once again be read in full.

Inscription	**Expanded Text**
D M	*Dis Manibus*
EGLECTAE AN	*Eglectae annos*
XXX H S SEC	*XXX hic sitae secus*
CRESCENTEM	*Crescentem*
F AN III ANTO	*filium annos III Antoninus*
STHEPAN CONIVGI	*Stephanus coniugi*
F C	*faciendum curavit*

Translation
TO THE SPIRITS OF THE DEAD
For Eglecta 30 years old
she lies here beside
Crescens
her 3-year-old son
Antonius Stephanus
set this up for his wife

The inscription is, as Lister noted, uniformly cut and well spaced within the panel. Spacing is marked with small triangular interpuncts, and ligatures are used for LE and NT. The name Stephanus in the penultimate line seems to have caused the stonecutter some difficulty: a ligature between the T and E letterforms indicates the addition of an H, here, to form STHEPAN. Most correct this to the name Stephanus.

The deceased are named as Eglecta and Crescens, a mother and her young son. Eglecta was 30 years old – that rounded number again! – when she passed away, while Crescens was 3 years old. There is a small note added in the third line to let us know the two have been buried together: Eglecta lies with her son in the grave. The tombstone has been erected by the head of the family, Antonius Stephanus, who clarifies at the end that he has created the monument for his wife. We are given no further information on their origins, though the name of the father in particular suggests possible Greek roots – the stonemason here has especially struggled with the correct spelling of Stephanus (STHEPAN).

The inscription occupies a central panel and is flanked by two winged figures. The figure on the left side has survived in much better condition than its weathered counterpart – his wings are clearly visible above his shoulders, and the childlike body shape makes it clearer that this figure is a Cupid. Both face the viewer, supporting the central panel with their adjacent arm. Cupid-like figures often appear on children's sarcophagi in the ancient world, often engaged in various activities like chariot racing. Here, the two small standing figures bring a sense of playfulness to the scene as well as perhaps hint towards the onward journey of the soul through their outspread wings.

FAMILY DINNERS

FLAVIUS CALLIMORPHUS

On a convivial memorial from Deva, a man and child enjoy an eternal dinner party together: unlike the tombstone of Martialis we have just seen, however, this child is not a slave but is a participant in the festivities.[41] The tombstone was recovered in the late nineteenth century: the grave site included two skeletons, a gold ring, and a bronze coin. The dinner scene takes up more than half of the 1.27-metre high stone. Underneath, a fairly uniformly carved inscription identifies the two figures as Flavius Callimorphus and Serapion.

<table>
<tr><td>Inscription</td><td>Expanded Text</td></tr>
<tr><td>D M</td><td>Dis Manibus</td></tr>
<tr><td>FL CALLIMOR</td><td>Flavi Callimorphi</td></tr>
<tr><td>PHI VIX ANI XXXXII</td><td>vixit annis XXXXII</td></tr>
<tr><td>ET SERAPIONI VIX</td><td>et Serapioni vixit</td></tr>
<tr><td>ANN IIIM VI THESA</td><td>annis III mensibus VI</td></tr>
<tr><td>EUS FRATRI ET FILIO</td><td>Thesaeus fratri et filio</td></tr>
<tr><td>F C</td><td>faciendum curavit</td></tr>
</table>

Translation
TO THE SPIRITS OF THE DEAD
For Flavius Callimorphus
who lived 42 years
and for Serapion
who lived 3 years and 6 months
Thesaeus set this up
for his brother and son

The names are an interesting insight into the people of Roman Deva, for all three names are Greek. Serapion is especially striking, derived from the Graeco-Egyptian god Serapis, whose worship as a god of healing was popular during the Roman Empire. Most accounts suggest this family unit were either traders or freedmen. There are a handful of inscriptions to or from individuals with Greek names in Deva: we have already encountered the tombstone of Curatia Dionysia in Chapter 4, while two altars have also survived from two Greek doctors, Antiochus and Hermogenes, which were written in Ancient Greek rather than Latin.[42] Here, no female names are provided for either the role of mother (to Serapion) or wife (of Flavius Callimorphus).

It is difficult to know for certain from the inscription whether Serapion was the son of Flavius Callimorphus or Thesaeus. The phrasing leaves the interpretation open though the scene on the tombstone itself, showing an affectionate moment between the two figures, seems to suggest the deceased were father and son. The older figure of Flavius reclines on the couch, propped up on his left elbow, looking relaxed. His head is damaged and the face no longer survives, but the remnants suggest he is slightly turned away from the viewer, looking towards the little figure of the child, Serapion. The child sits on his father's lap in the middle of the couch. His left arm gestures outwards towards the father, while in his right hand he holds a cup. Although it is worn away, it is possible to see the father's right hand resting on Serapion's shoulder. This glimpse into family life creates a touching memorial.

Pictured in front of the couch is an upright two-handled amphora, its general shape suggesting a fairly typical container for wine. Next to it, a bird perches on a three-legged table. Birds frequently appear on ancient monuments to the dead. In Ancient Egypt, funerary art often depicted the *ba* (), a bird with the head of a human, flitting around and away from the deceased's body. In the Ancient

Fig. 5.7 Tombstone of Flavius Callimorphus and Serapion, on display at the Grosvenor Museum, Chester.

Greek world, birds are often found on the gravestones of children – one of the most well-known examples is perhaps the beautiful marble 'Dove Stele' from the mid-fifth century BC, which shows a young girl affectionately clutching two doves. Children often kept small animals or birds as pets – and many toy animals have also been recovered from the grave sites of children. Here, on our tombstone, the bird could be a symbol of the soul's onward journey – or it could be the toy or pet of young Serapion, accompanying him even in death.

RESTITA AND MARTIA

On another lively tombstone from Deva, two young sisters, Restita and Martia, are also shown enjoying a dinner party together.[43] The stone was recovered from Chester's north wall and has been fairly badly damaged. It has been broken into ten fragments of varying sizes: the central figures of the two girls no longer survive on the monument beyond two reclining left arms, though fortunately their faces have been recovered separately. The inscription is partially preserved.

Inscription	**Expanded Text**
D M	*Dis Manibus*
RESTITAE V ANN	*Restitae vixit annos*
VII ET M	*VII et Martiae*
ARTIAE V ANN III	*vixit annos III*
[.] AR[.] NTES	*parentes*
[....]	*[....]*

Translation
TO THE SPIRITS OF THE DEAD
For Restita who lived 7 years
and for Martia
who lived 3 years
Their parents
[....]

The composition of the scene is fairly typical of the 'dinner party' type we have encountered so far: the deceased are shown reclining on a central high-backed couch. The visible figure leans on their left arm, which is bent at the elbow. Both the pillow and mattress beneath the figure are still visible. In front of the couch is a three-legged table. Behind the couch hangs a large seashell. As we saw in Chapter 4, seashells on a tombstone are often thought to represent the long journey the soul must take across the sea to reach the underworld but could also be considered a symbol of the goddess Venus. The recovered stone faces from the monument show two young girls with happy features and neatly styled hair.

The inscription underneath the scene preserves the names and ages of the two little girls. Restita was 7 when she passed away, while Martia was only 3 years old. We know that both mother and father were listed as dedicators through the use of *parentes*, the Latin word for parents, in the final partially visible line of the surviving text. The depiction of the two sisters together, enjoying each other's company in an eternal dinner party, perhaps offered a small comfort to the parents as they came to terms with their dreadful loss.

Notes

Introduction
 1. Virgil *Aeneid* 6.325–30.
 2. Rogan (2006), 77.
 3. Toynbee (1971), 43–4.
 4. For those interested in the details of the conquest, Shotter's overview in his 2004 *Roman Britain* book is well worth consulting.
 5. Harding (2016), 7.
 6. Delattre (2011), 609.
 7. Harding (2016), 8–10.
 8. Harding (2016), 8.
 9. Fendel (2025), 9

Chapter 1
 1. See Mattingly (2006) for detailed accounts of the units stationed in the province over the duration of the Roman occupation.
 2. Hope (2003), 80.
 3. Hope (2003), 87.
 4. RIB3218.
 5. RIB619.
 6. RIB194.
 7. Hope (2018), 10.
 8. RIB1667.
 9. Clayton (1855), 58.
10. Scherer (1955).
11. ILS 2732.
12. Birley (1988), 152.
13. RIB1350.
14. See esp. Haeussler (1994), 62 onwards on Celtic onomastics.
15. *Tab. Lond. Bloomberg* WT48.
16. RIB360.
17. Camden (1695), 606.
18. Mattingly (2006).
19. Scheidel (1992), 281–97.
20. Tomlin (2018), 207.
21. RIB258.
22. RIB671.
23. RIB256.
24. Birley (1953), 113.

25. RIB292.
26. Hesiod *Theogony* 720–5.
27. RIB497.
28. RIB523.
29. Malone (2005), 223; see also the commentary and notes on RIB523.
30. RIB522.
31. Diodorus Siculus, *Library of History* 5.28.2–3 (transl. Oldfather 1939).
32. See esp. Sim & Kaminski (2012) *Roman Imperial Armour*.
33. For discussion of this custom along with discussion on differentiation between slaves and children, see Masséglia (2015) *Body Language in Hellenistic Art and Society*, Oxford.
34. Fields (2005); evidence of the practice among Roman auxiliaries in Britain includes two 'trophy' heads excavated at Vindolanda (one whose teeth indicate a north-western British origin).
35. Diodorus Siculus *Library of History* 5.29.4–5 (transl. Oldfather 1939).
36. RIB369.
37. Allason-Jones (2005), 20.
38. See esp. the discussion in Edward (1849).
39. Hope (2018), 35–49.
40. Phang (2007), 286–305.
41. Raybould (1997), 363.
42. RIB363.
43. RIB359.
44. RIB363, RIB371, RIB372, RIB373, RIB374, RIB375, RIB377.
45. RIB373.
46. Allason-Jones (2005), 56.
47. RIB620.
48. Tomlin (2008), 135.

Chapter 2
1. Alcock (2006), 37.
2. Campbell (2005), s.v. *principales*.
3. RIB544.
4. RIB1742.
5. Not to be confused with *cornicen*, the trumpeter.
6. Austin (2010), 113–14.
7. Breeze (1969), 119–20.
8. Birley (1953), 76; Dobson and Mann (1973), 200.
9. Alcock (2006), 38.
10. See Parker & Watson (2012) and Sage (2014).
11. Campbell (2018), 50.
12. Rather effectively described by Tomlin (2018), 20 as a 'swagger-stick, which symbolised his power to flog defaulters'.
13. Pliny the Elder *Natural History* 14.3.
14. Prideaux (1676); Sturdy & Moorcraft (1999).
15. Hassall (1973), 233–4; Cooley (2018), 236.
16. RIB19.

17. See especially Simon Elliott (2023) *Roman Special Forces and Special Ops: Speculatores, Exploratores, Protectores, and Areani in the Service of Rome*, Pen & Sword Books (Barnsley).
18. Tomlin (2018), 266.
19. RIB200.
20. Huskinson (1994), 23.
21. Zelnick-Abramovitz (2018).
22. Hayward (2016).
23. Phillips (1975), 105; Hayward (2016), 362.
24. Tacitus *Annals* 14.31 (transl. Jackson).
25. Cassius Dio *Roman History* 62.2.
26. Tacitus *Annals* 14.32.
27. Camulodunum burned so ferociously that it left what is known by archaeologists as the 'Boudiccan destruction horizon'.
28. RIB2213.
29. Tomlin (2018), 64.
30. Historic Environment Scotland SM1601 Ardoch.
31. RIB1618.
32. Sander (1958); Davies (1969b); Nutton (1969).
33. Nutton (1969), 262.
34. Allason-Jones (1999), 134.
35. Gilson (1978); *ingenuus* carried the meaning 'freeborn'.
36. *Tab. Vindol.* 154.
37. See e.g. Philostratus *Imagines* 1.6.5–7.
38. *Diseases of Women* II 76.
39. Caesar *Gallic Wars* 5.12.
40. RIB1288.
41. Hodgson, Britton & Brayley (1812), 153.
42. Millar/Burton (2012) s.v. *equites*.
43. Campbell (2012) s.v. *tribuni militum*.
44. Campbell (2012) s.v. *tribuni militum*.
45. Tomlin (2018), 199.
46. Allason-Jones (2005), 47.
47. Foubert (2013) 399–400.
48. See esp. Anderson (1984); Schleiermacher (1984); Shotter (2007).
49. *Brit.* 54.13, RIB 2411.84, *Brit.* 49.6; RIB957.
50. RIB935.
51. The ideal – and likely theoretical – sizes being 512 and 1024 (see esp. Zahariade 2012).
52. Collinson (1791), 12.
53. Mann (2002), 228–9.
54. RIB3185.
55. *De Bello Gallico* 2.24; cf. 8.25.
56. BRIT 39.5.
57. RIB521.
58. Maxfield (2012), s.v. Military Standards.
59. RIB665.
60. RIB1171.

61. Birley (2012), 1–16. Constructions on the Antonine wall began *c*.AD 140 though it is uncertain whether the cohort were the first or second garrison – nevertheless, they were back in Magna by the early AD 160s.
62. Birley (1953), 81–2.
63. Mattingly (2006); Eckardt et al. (2014), 356; Tomlin (2018), 224; Kempen (2022), 49.
64. RIB3354.
65. RIB1154.
66. Birley (2012).
67. Tomlin (2018), 224.
68. Recorded at Arbeia on the *Notitia Dignitatum* (xl.22) in the fourth century; Birley suggests they may well have been there since the early third century. Birley (1971/88), 202 n.6.

Chapter 3
1. RIB155.
2. North (2016), s.v. priests.
3. τρυφή.
4. RIB12; BM 1852,0806.2.
5. Historic England Monument 405276.
6. De La Bédoyère (2015), 43.
7. Grasby & Tomlin (2002), 66–7.
8. Tacitus *Annals* 14.38.
9. Tacitus *Annals* 3.42.
10. RIB108; Hassall (1982), 67–8.
11. RIB1436.
12. Tomlin (2018), 263; Birley (1979), 208; cf. RIB1436 for note by Wright.
13. Carroll (2006), 44–8.
14. RIB1064 (Victor) and RIB1065 (Regina).
15. Wilson (2005) s.v. Mauretania.
16. Pliny the Elder *Natural History* 8.67.
17. Croom (2020).
18. Smith (1959), 207.
19. Ivleva (2020), 254 who also quotes Skinner (2014), 349 'slaves who had been boyfriends were warmly remembered'.
20. Almost 4,000 portraits have been collated and studied since 2012 as part of the 'Palmyra Portrait Project'.
21. Heyn & Raja (2019), 39–51; Stauffer (2012), 89–98.
22. See esp. Raja (2022).
23. RIB749.
24. cf. for example *CIL* 13, 06910, which ends with FRAT POSV A V (*fratres posuerunt ave vale*) 'his brothers set up this monument, hail and farewell!'.
25. RIB747.
26. Allason-Jones (2017), 5; Allason-Jones (2005), 47.
27. RIB955.
28. Haverfield (1893), 312.
29. Kruschwitz (2015), 295–6.
30. Aldhouse-Green (2018), 166.

31. De la Bédoyère (2015), 182.
32. Nash-Williams (1950), 172.
33. Woolf (1996), 28.
34. RIB955.
35. Laurence and Trifilo (2012), find 1,790 to analyse in their study; cf. Bennett (2020), 63 who lists 1,805 examples from across the major provinces.
36. Lassère (1973), 127.
37. Kruschwitz (2015), 296.
38. Ellis (1893), 615.
39. De la Bédoyère (2015), 183.
40. RIB3045.

Chapter 4
 1. Historic England 26499.
 2. HER 903 Roman cremation cemetery, South Shields; cf. Snape (1994).
 3. RIB1065.
 4. The script is transliterated by RIB as RGYN° BT ḤRY BR ᶜTᵓ ḤBL.
 5. Perry (2014), 69.
 6. Perry (2014), 90–1.
 7. Allason-Jones (2005), 14.
 8. Laurence (2012), 124.
 9. Carroll (2012), 292–3.
10. Rothe (2012), 240; Croom (2020).
11. Carroll (2012), 296.
12. Carroll (2012), 296 argues it should not be interpreted as a visual sign of 'Celtic-ness' – though it is hard to imagine that it was not a deliberately chosen detail, especially if it was no longer common in Roman-era contemporary fashion.
13. Carroll (2012), 297.
14. Dixon (2004), 65.
15. Snape (1994), 54–5.
16. Smith (1959), 203–10.
17. RIB639.
18. Watkin (1884), 127–8.
19. Third declension nominative singular endings can include *-a, -e, -ī, -ō, -y, -c, -l, -n, -r, -s, -t,* or *-x.*
20. Based on the comparative Latin word *trico* ('mischief-maker') which has the genitive form *triconis.*
21. Webster (1975), 18.
22. *Notitia Dignitatum* 40.
23. Birney (1990), 58.
24. RIB3221 calls it the first British occurrence of a 'widespread formula'.
25. TM180705 and TM180693 (Dacia).
26. Corinium Museum 2016.1/1.
27. RIB562.
28. Stewart (2009), 257.
29. They are described carrying out both actions in textual sources (Pausanias 8.2.7; Philostratus *Imagines* 1.25).

30. RIB563.
31. RIB682.
32. The building is now known as 'The House of Venus in the Shell'.
33. Getty Museum: Aphrodite and the Gods of Love – Roman Venus.
34. RIB688.
35. Allason-Jones (2005), 12–13.
36. RIB687.
37. Kaster (2010).
38. Tomlin (2018), 237.
39. RIB959; Hodgson (1832), 419.
40. Virgil *Georgics* 1.212.
41. RIB1828.
42. Vermote (2016), 138.
43. Campbell (1978), 153–66.
44. RIB1795.
45. e.g. 1 Peter 1:19, 1 Timothy 6:14; cf. Augustine's *Confessions* 10.1; Birley (1948) and R.P.W as noted in RIB1795.
46. *Pro Plancio* 6.15.
47. Vermote (2016), 138.
48. RIB250.
49. Tomlin (2018), 253.
50. Interestingly, *bene merens* was also a popular way of commemorating gladiators on epitaphs across the empire as a way of emphasising how bravely they had faced their duty in the arena – see Hope (2000), 105.
51. BM 1862.0423.1.
52. Hemelrijk (2020), 116.
53. Nuorluoto (2023), 93–4.
54. RIB263.

Chapter 5
1. Pliny the Elder, *Natural History* 7.15.
2. *Tusculan Disputations* 1.39.
3. *Tusculan Disputations* 1.39.
4. RIB690.
5. RIB684.
6. Kruschwitz (2013).
7. RIB758.
8. Minns (1942) noted on RIB758.
9. Homer *Odyssey* 24.5.
10. Homer *Odyssey* 10.504*ff.*
11. RIB961.
12. Ferguson (1886), 127.
13. Wright & Phillips (1975), 59.
14. Ferguson (1886), 128.
15. Morehouse (2024), 104.
16. RIB1747.
17. RIB784.

18. Birley (1980), 113.
19. RIB932.
20. Haverfield (1913), 191.
21. Birley (1947), 175–6.
22. RIB1180, RIB1181, RIB1182.
23. Taylor and Birley (1938).
24. RIB1880.
25. RIB560.
26. Tomlin (2018), 238.
27. Rawson (2012).
28. Allason-Jones (2004), 282.
29. RIB3072; Henig & Tomlin (2008).
30. See esp. the discussion of the image in the entry for RIB3072.
31. RIB937.
32. Compare Townley's sketch of a Greek tombstone, which translates the Greek name into Latin as 'Ylas' (British Museum 2010,5006. 1877.29).
33. Dry (2012); Bremmer (2000).
34. Tomlin (2018), 207.
35. RIB685.
36. RIB3290.
37. Tomlin (2018), 232.
38. RIB686.
39. Phillips (1976), 102.
40. RIB695.
41. RIB558.
42. RIB3161 & RIB461.
43. RIB566.

Appendix 1

Commonly Used Abbreviations

A/AN + numeral	*annus*	year
	annos [+ numeral]	[number] years
ANNOR + numeral	*annorum [+ numeral]*	of [number] years
B M	*bene merens/bene merenti*	well-deserving
>	*centurio*	centurion
C + place	*civis [+ place]*	citizen of [place]
C	*coniunx*	wife
COH	*cohors*	Cohort
COH P	*cohors prima*	First Cohort
D + numeral	*dies [+ numeral]*	day/days
D + place	*domo [+ place]*	his/her home was [place]
D M	*Dis Manibus*	To the spirits of the dead
D I M	*Dis Inferis Manibus*	To the spirits of the dead below
D M S	*Dis Manibus sacrum*	To the sacred spirits of the dead
D S	*de suo*	with his/her own money
EQ	*eques*	horseman (cavalry)
F	*filius*	son
	filia	daughter
F C	*faciendum curavit*	he/she took care to set this up
	faciendum curaverunt	they took care to set this up
FIL	*filius*	son
	filia	daughter
H E	*hic est*	here is
H S E	*hic situs est*	here he/she lies
L	*libertus*	freedman
	liberta	freedwoman
LEG	*legio*	legion
M + numeral	*mensis*	month
	menses [+ numeral]	[number] months
M/MIL/ML	*miles*	soldier

NAT + location	*natione [+ location]*	from the __________ people
P	*posuit*	he/she placed
	posuerunt	they placed
P C	*ponendum curavit*	he/she took care to set this up
PAT	*pater*	father
PO	*posuit*	he/she placed
	posuerunt	they placed
S T T L	*sit terra tibi levis*	may the earth lie light upon you
STI/STIP/STP + numeral	*stipendiorum [+ numeral]*	with [number] years' service
V	*vixit*	he/she lived
V/VET	*veteranus*	military veteran
VIX	*vixit*	he/she lived

Appendix 2

Roman Place Names

Aesica	Great Chesters (Hadrian's Wall)
Alauna	Maryport
Aquae Sulis	Bath
Arbeia	South Shields
Banna	Birdoswald (Hadrian's Wall)
Bremenium	High Rochester
Brocolitia	Carrawburgh (Hadrian's Wall)
Burrium	Usk
Camboglanna	Castlesteads (Hadrian's Wall)
Camulodunum	Colchester
Castra Exploratorum	Netherby
Cilurnum	Chesters (Hadrian's Wall)
Coccium	Wigan
Condercum	Benwell (Hadrian's Wall)
Coria/Corstopitum	Corbridge
Corinium Dobunnorum	Cirencester
Danum	Doncaster
Derventione	Papcastle
Deva Victrix	Chester
Dubris	Dover
Eboracum	York
Glevum	Gloucester
Isca Dumnoniorum	Exeter
Isca Silurum / Augusta	Carleon
Lindum	Lincoln
Londinium	London
Longovicium	Lanchester
Luguvalium	Carlisle (central)
Maglona	Wigton / Old Carlisle

Magnis/Magna	Carvoran (Hadrian's Wall)
Maia	Bowness-on-Salway (Hadrian's Wall)
Onnum/Hunnum	Halton Chesters (Hadrian's Wall)
Petriana/Uxelodunum	Stanwix (Hadrian's Wall)
Pons Aelius	Newcastle upon Tyne (Hadrian's Wall)
Portus Abonae	Sea Mills
Ratae Corieltauvorum	Leicester
Segedunum	Wallsend (Hadrian's Wall)
Segontium	Caernarfon
Trimontium	Newstead
Vercovicium	Housesteads (Hadrian's Wall)
Verteris/Verterae	Brough-under-Stainmore
Vindobala	Rudchester (Hadrian's Wall)
Vindolanda	Chesterholme
Vinovia	Binchester
Viroconium	Wroxeter
Voreda	Penrith

Bibliography

Adams, G. & R. Tober (2007) *Romano-British Tombstones between the 1st and 3rd centuries AD: epigraphy, gender, and family relations*, Oxford.

Alcock, J. (2006) *Life in Roman Britain*, Cheltenham.

Aldhouse-Green, M. (2018) *Sacred Britannia: The Gods and Rituals of Roman Britain*, London.

Allason-Jones, L. (1999) 'Healthcare in the Roman North', *Britannia* 30: 133–46.

Allason-Jones, L. (2004) 'The Family in Roman Britain' in M. Todd (ed.) *A Companion to Roman Britain*, Hoboken NJ: 273–287.

Allason-Jones, L. (2005) *Women in Roman Britain*, York.

Allason-Jones, L. (2017) 'Women, the military, and *patria potestas* in Roman Britain' in N. Hodgson, P. Bidwell & J. Schachtmann (eds) *Roman Frontier Studies 2009: Proceedings of the XXI International Congress of Roman Frontier Studies*, Oxford: 3–8.

Anderson, A. (1984) *Roman Military Tombstones*, Aylesbury.

Austin, J. (2010) *Writers and Writing in the Roman Army at Dura Europos*, PhD thesis, University of Birmingham.

Bennett, L. (2020) *Global patterns of commemoration in Roman epitaphs: a quantitative spatial analysis of the most common formulae*, PhD thesis, University of Kent.

Birley, A. (1980) *The People of Roman Britain*, London.

Birley, A. (1988) *Septimius Severus: The African Emperor*, London.

Birley, A. (2012) 'The Cohors I Hamiorum in Britain', *Acta Classica* LV: 1–16.

Birley, E. (1947) 'Old Penrith and its problems', *Transactions of Cumberland and Westmorland Antiquarian and Archaeological Society* 47: 166–182.

Birley, E. (1953) *Roman Britain and the Roman Army: Collected Papers*, Kendal.

Birley, E. (1988) 'Pannonians in Roman Britain', *Zeitschrift für Papyrologie und Epigraphik* 73: 151–155.

Birney, M. (1990) *The cult of Venus in Roman Britain*, PhD thesis, Michigan State University.

Breeze, D. (1969) *The immunes and principales of the Roman army*, PhD thesis, Durham University.

Breeze, D. (2016) *The Roman Army*, London.

Breeze, D. (2023) *Frontiers of the Roman Empire: the Hinterland of Hadrian's Wall*, Bicester.

Bremmer, J. (2000) 'Fosterage, kinship and the circulation of children in ancient Greece', *Dialogos: Hellenic Studies Review* 6: 1–20.

Camden, W. (1695) *Camden's Britannia: newly translated into English*, London.

Campbell, B. (1978) 'The marriage of soldiers under the empire', *The Journal of Roman Studies* 68: 153–166.

Campbell, B. (2005) '*Principales*', Brill's New Pauly, Leiden.

Campbell, B. (2012) '*tribuni militum*' in S. Hornblower, A. Spawforth & E. Eidinow (eds), *Oxford Classical Dictionary*, Oxford.

Campbell, D. (2018) 'Auxiliary centurions: the forgotten officers', *Ancient Warfare* XI, 6: 50–53.

Carroll, M. (2006) *Spirits of the Dead: Roman Funerary Commemoration in Western Europe*, Oxford.

Carroll, M. (2012) 'The Insignia of Women: Dress, Gender and Identity on the Roman Funerary Monument of Regina from Arbeia', *Archaeological Journal* 169: 281–311.

Clayton (1855) 'Account of Excavations at the Mile Castle of Cawfields on the Roman Wall', *Archaeologia Aeliana* 4: 54–59.

Collinson, J. (1791) *The History and Antiquities of the County of Somerset*, Bath.

Cooley, A. (2018) 'Monumental Latin Inscriptions from Roman Britain in the Ashmolean Museum Collection', *Society for the Promotion of Roman Studies* 49: 225–249.

Coombe, P., M. Henig, F. Grew & K. Hayward (2015) *Roman Sculpture from London and the South East*, Oxford.

Croom, A. (2020) 'The Victor Tombstone' *Tyne & Wear Archives and Museums* [https://blog. twmuseums.org.uk/the-victor-tombstone/]

Croom, A. (2020) 'The Regina Tombstone' *Tyne & Wear Archives and Museums*.

Crummy, P. (1993) 'The Cemeteries of Roman Colchester' in P. Crummy (ed.) *Colchester Archaeological Report 9: Excavations of Roman and later cemeteries, churches and monastic sites in Colchester 1971–88*, Colchester Archaeological Trust: 257–276.

Davies, R.W. (1969) 'The medici of the Roman armed forces', *Epigraphische Studien* 8: 83–99.

De La Bédoyère, G. (2015) *Real Lives of Roman Britain*, New Haven CT.

Delattre, V. (2011) 'The ritual representation of the body during the late Iron Age in northern France', in T. Moore & X-L. Armada (eds) *Atlantic Europe in the First Millenium BC: Crossing the Divide*, Oxford: 608–14.

Dixon, K. & P. Southern (1992) *The Roman Cavalry*, London.

Dixon, S. (2004) 'Exemplary housewife or luxurious slut: cultural representations of women in the Roman economy', in F. McHardy & E. Marshall (eds) *Women's Influence on Classical Civilisation*, London: 56–74.

Dobson, B. & J.C. Mann (1973) 'The Roman army in Britain and Britons in the Roman army', *Britannia* 4: 191–205.

Dry, D. (2012) 'Fostering, foster-child' in A. Erskine, D. Hollander & A. Papaconstantinou (eds), *The Encyclopaedia of Ancient History*, Hoboken NJ.

Eckardt, H., G. Muldner & M. Lewis (2014) 'People on the move in Roman Britain', *World Archaeology* 46: 4, 534–550.

Edward, L.J. (1847) 'Roman Remains found lately at Caerleon', *Archaeologia Cambrensis* 14: 73–82.

Ellis, R. (1893) 'The Roman Inscription from Carlisle', *The Academy* 42: 615.

Fendel, V. (2025) 'Crossing thresholds: lexicalization and performance of memory in early imperial funerary inscriptions from Sicily', *Lexis*: 1–26.

Ferguson, R.S. (1886) 'On a Roman inscribed tombstone found in Carlisle', *Archaeologia Aeliana* 11: 127–130.

Fields (2005) 'Headhunters of the Roman Army' in A. Hopkins & M. Wyke (eds) *Roman Bodies: antiquity to the eighteenth century*, London.

Foubert, L. (2013) 'Female travellers in Roman Britain: Vibia Pacata and Julia Lucilla', in E.A. Hemelrijk & G. Woolf (eds), *Women and the Roman City in the West*, Leiden: 391–403.

Gilson, A. (1978) 'A doctor at Housesteads', *Archaeologia Aeliana* 6: 162–65.

Grasby, R.D. & O. Tomlin (2002) 'The Sepulchral Monument of the Procurator C. Julius Classicianus', *Britannia* 33: 43–75.

Haeussler, R. (1994) 'The Romanisation of the *civitas Vangionum*', *Bulletin of the Institute of Archaeology London* 15: 41–104.

Harding, D. (2016) *Death and Burial in Iron Age Britain*, Oxford.

Hassall, M. (1973) 'Roman soldiers in Roman London' in D.E. Strong (ed.) *Archaeological Theory & Practice*, London: 231–237.

Hassall, M. (1982) 'Epigraphic evidence for the auxiliary garrison at Cirencester', in J. Wacher & A. McWhirr (eds) *Early Roman Occupation at Cirencester*, Cirencester: 67–71.

Hassall, M. & R.S.O. Tomlin (1996) 'Roman Britain in 1995: II. Inscriptions', *Britannia* 27: 439–57.

Haverfield, F.J. (1893) 'Three notable Roman inscriptions', *Archaeological Journal* 50: 308–321.

Haverfield, F.J. (1913) 'Voreda the Roman fort at Plumpton Wall', *Transactions of Cumberland and Westmorland Antiquarian and Archaeological Society* 13: 177–198.

Hayward, K. (2016) 'A Geological Link between the Facilis Monument at Colchester and First-century Army Tombstones from the Rhineland Frontier', *Britannia* 37: 359–363.

Hemelrijk, E. (2020) *Women and Society in the Roman World*, Cambridge.

Henig, M., G. Webster & T. Blaag (2004) *Roman Sculpture from the North West Midlands*, Oxford.

Henig, M. & R.S.O. Tomlin (2008) 'The sculptural stone', in Simmonds *et al. Life and Death in a Roman City: Excavation of a Roman Cemetery with a Mass Grave at 120–122 London Road, Gloucester*, Oxford: 116–118.

Heyn, M.K. (2010) 'Gesture and Identity in the art of Palmyra', *American Journal of Archaeology* 113: 631–61.

Heyn, M.K. & R. Raja (2019) 'Male Dress Habits in Roman Period Palmyra' in M. Cifarelli (ed.) *Fashioned Selves: Dress and Identity in Antiquity*, Oxford: 39–51.

Hodgson, J., J. Britton & E.W. Brayley (1812) *The Beauty of England and Wales*, London.

Hodgson, J. (1832) 'Account of two Roman inscriptions', *Archaeologia Aeliana* 2: 419–420.

Holder, P. (1982) *The Roman Army in Britain*, London.

Hope, V. (2003) 'Remembering Rome: memory, funerary monuments and the Roman soldier', in H. Williams (ed.) *Archaeologies of Remembrance: Death and Memory in Past Societies*, New York: 113–140.

Hope, V. (2003) 'Trophies and tombstones: commemorating the Roman soldier', *World Archaeology* 35: 79–97.

Hope, V. (2018) '"Dulce et decorum est pro patria mori": the practical and symbolic treatment of the Roman war dead', *Mortality* 23: 35–49.

Huskinson, J. (1994) *Roman Sculptures from Eastern England*, Oxford.

Ivleva, T. (2020) 'Coming out of the provincial closet: Masculinity, sexuality, and same-sex sexual relations amongst Roman soldiers in the European north-west, first–third centuries AD' in T. Ivleva & R. Collins (eds), *Un-Roman sex: gender, sexuality, and lovemaking in the Roman provinces and frontiers*, Abingdon: 241–273.

Kaster, R. (2010), 'Values and Virtues, Roman' in M. Gagarin & E. Fantham (eds) *The Oxford Encyclopedia of Ancient Greece and Rome*, New York.

Kempen, M. (2022) *Socialising soldiers in the north: military communities and Romanisation in Britain 43 AD–212 AD*, PhD thesis, Universiteit Leiden.

Keppie, L. (1991) *Understanding Roman Inscriptions*, Baltimore.

Kruschwitz, P. (2013) 'Hope and despair in Roman Britain', The Petrified Muse blog [https://thepetrifiedmuse.blog/2013/08/10/hope-and-despair-in-roman-britain/]

Kruschwitz, P. (2015) *Undying Voices: The Poetry of Roman Britain*, Reading.

Lassère, J-M. (1973) 'Recherches Sur La Chronologie Des Épitaphes Païennes de l'Africa', *Antiquités Africaine* 7: 7–152.

Laurence, R. (2012) *Roman Archaeology for Historians*, London.

Laurence, R. & F. Trifilo (2012) 'Vixit plus minus. Commemorating the age of the dead: towards a Roman familial life course?' in M. Harlow & L. Larsson Loven (eds) *Families in the Roman and Late Antique World*, London: 23–40.

Lavan, M. (2019) 'The army and the spread of Roman citizenship', *Journal of Roman Studies* 109: 27–69.

Liu, J. (2019) 'Freedmen and Freedwomen' in A. Erskine, D. Hollander & A. Papaconstantinou (eds), *The Encyclopaedia of Ancient History*, Hoboken NJ.

Malone, S. (2005) *Legio XX Valeria Victrix: a prosopographical and historical study*, PhD thesis, University of Nottingham.

Mann, J.C. (2002) 'The Settlement of Veterans Discharged from Auxiliary Units Stationed in Britain', *Britannia* 33: 183–188.

Masséglia, J. (2015) *Body Language in Hellenistic Art and Society*, Oxford.

Mattingly, D. (2006) *An Imperial Possession: Britain in the Roman Empire*, London.

Maxfield, V.A & B. Dobson (2006) *Inscriptions of Roman Britain* (4th edition), London.

Maxfield, V.A. (2012) 'Military standards' in A. Erskine, D. Hollander & A. Papaconstantinou (eds), *Encyclopaedia of Ancient History*, Hoboken NJ.

Merrifield, R.(1983) *London: City of the Romans*, Berkeley CA.

Millar, F. & G. Burton (2012) '*equites* in the imperial period', in S. Hornblower, A. Spawforth & E. Eidinow (eds), *Oxford Classical Dictionary*, Oxford.

Morehouse, L. (2024) *Recontextualising the boy with grapes stelae of Roman Egypt: authenticity, connectivity, and memory*, PhD thesis, University of Amsterdam.

Nash-Williams, V.E. (1950) *The Early Christian Monuments of Wales*, Cardiff.

North, J. (2016) 'Priests' in S. Hornblower, A. Spawforth & E. Eidinow (eds), *Oxford Classical Dictionary*, Oxford.

Nuorluoto, T. (2023) *Latin Female Cognomina: A Study on the Personal Names of Roman Women*, Helsinki.

Nutton, V. (1969) 'Medicine and the Roman army: a further consideration', *Medical History* 13: 260–270.

Parker, H. & G.R. Watson (2012) *The Roman legions*, Cambridge.

Perry, M. (2014) *Gender, Manumission, and the Roman Freedwoman*, Cambridge.

Phang, S.E. (2007) 'Military documents, language and literacy' in P. Erdkamp (ed.), *A companion to the Roman army*, 286–305.

Phillips, E.J. (1975) 'The Gravestone of M. Favonius Facilis at Colchester', *Britannia* 6: 102–105.

Phillips, E.J. (1976) 'A Workshop of Roman Sculptors at Carlisle', *Britannia* 7: 101–108.

Prideaux, H. (1676) *Marmora Oxoniensia ex Arundelliais, Seldenianis aliisque conflata*, Oxford.

Raja R. (2022) 'Revisiting the Palmyrene Banqueting Tesserae: Conceptualization, Production, Usage, and Meaning of the Palmyrene Tesserae – Perspectives for a New Corpus', in R. Raja (ed.) *The small stuff of the Palmyrenes: Studies in Palmyrene Archaeology and History* 5, Turnhout: 5–67.

Rawson, B. (2012) '*vernae*' in A. Erskine, D. Hollander & A. Papaconstantinou (eds), *The Encyclopaedia of Ancient History*, Hoboken NJ.

Raybould, M. (1997) *A study of inscribed material from Roman Britain*, PhD thesis, University of Wales Newport.

Rogan, J. (2007) *Reading Roman Inscriptions*, Stroud.

Rothe, U. (2012) 'Dress and cultural identity in the Roman Empire', in M. Harlow (ed.) *Dress and Identity*, Oxford: 59–68.

Sage, M. (2014), '*Centurio*', A. Erskine, D. Hollander & A. Papaconstantinou (eds), *Encyclopaedia of Ancient History*, Hoboken NJ.

Sander, E. (1958) 'Zur Rangordnung des römischen Heeres; der duplicarius', *Historia* 9: 239–43.

Scheidel, W. (1992) 'Inschriftenstatistik und die Frage des Rekrutierungsalters römischer Soldaten', *Chiron* 22: 281–297.

Scherer, A. (1955) 'Die keltisch-germanischen Namensgleichungen', *Corolla Linguistica* 199–210.

Schleiermacher, M. (1984) *Romische Reitergrabsteine: Die Kaiserzeitlichen Reliefs des triumphierenden Reiters*, Bonn.

Shotter, D.C.A. (2007) 'A Roman tombstone from Lancaster', *Contrebis* 31: 23–28.

Sim, D. & J. Kaminski (2012) *Roman imperial armour: the production of early imperial military armour*, Oxford.

Smith, D.J. (1959) 'A Palmyrene sculptor at South Shields', *Archaeologia Aeliana* 37: 203–210.

Snape, M.E. (1994) 'An Excavation in the Roman cemetery at South Shields', *Archaeologia Aeliana* 22: 43–66.

Stauffer, A. (2012) 'Dressing the Dead in Palmyra in the Second and Third Centuries AD', in M. Carroll & J.P. Wild (eds) *Dressing the Dead in Classical Antiquity*, Stroud: 89–98.

Stewart, P. (2009) 'Totenmahl reliefs in the northern provinces: a case-study in imperial sculpture', *Journal of Roman Archaeology* 22: 253–274.

Sturdy, D. & N. Moorcraft (1999) 'Christopher Wren and Oxford's Garden of Antiquities', *Minerva* 25–28.

Taylor, M.V. & E. Birley (1938) 'Roman Britain in 1937: II. Inscriptions', *Journal of Roman Studies* 28: 199–206.

Tomlin, R.S.O. (2011) 'Writing and Communication' in L. Allason-Jones (ed), *Artefacts in Roman Britain: Their Purpose and Use*, Cambridge: 133–152

Tomlin, R.S.O. (2018) *Britannia Romana: Roman Inscriptions and Roman Britain*, Oxford.

Toynbee, J.M.C. (1971) *Death and Burial in the Roman World*, London.

Vermote, K. (2016) 'The macula servitutis of Roman freedmen', *Revue Belge de Philologie et d'Histoire* 94: 131–164.

Wacher, J. (1995) *The Towns of Roman Britain* (second edition), London.

Watkin, W. (1884) 'Roman Inscriptions found in Britain in 1884', *Archaeological Journal* 42: 141–158.

Webster, G. (1975) *The Cornovii*, London.

Wilson, (2005) 'Mauretania' in S. Hornblower, A. Spawforth & E. Eidinow (eds), *Oxford Classical Dictionary*, Oxford.

Woolf, G. (1996) 'Monumental writing and the expansion of Roman society in the early empire', *Journal of Roman Studies* 86: 22–39.

Wright, R.P. & E.J. Phillips (1975) *Catalogue of the Roman inscribed and sculptured stones in Carlisle Museum Tullie House*, Carlisle.

Zahariade, M. (2012) 'Roman cavalry' in A. Erskine, D. Hollander & A. Papaconstantinou (eds), *The Encyclopaedia of Ancient History*, Hoboken NJ.

Zelnick-Abramowitz, R. (2018) 'Manumission: Greek and Roman', in A. Erskine, D. Hollander & A. Papaconstantinou (eds) *Encyclopaedia of Ancient History*, Hoboken NJ.

Index

Dear Reader,

We hope you have enjoyed this book, but why not share your views on social media? You can also follow our pages to see more about our other products: facebook.com/penandswordbooks or follow us on X @penswordbooks

You can also view our products at www.pen-and-sword.co.uk (UK and ROW) or www.penandswordbooks.com (North America).

To keep up to date with our latest releases and online catalogues, please sign up to our newsletter at: www.pen-and-sword.co.uk/newsletter

If you would like a printed catalogue with our latest books, then please email: enquiries@pen-and-sword.co.uk or telephone: 01226 734555 (UK and ROW) or email: uspen-and-sword@casematepublishers.com or telephone: (610) 853-9131 (North America).

We respect your privacy and we will only use personal information to send you information about our products.

Thank you!